500
traditional quilts

500
traditional quilts

Karey Patterson Bresenhan, Juror

LARK

EDITORS
Amanda Carestio
Dawn Dillingham

DESIGNER
Kathleen Holmes

COVER DESIGNER
Igor Satanovsky

FRONT COVER
Sharon Schamber
Spirit of Mother Earth, 2008

Keiko Miyauchi
Tree of Life, 2009

Marilyn Badger
Super Star, 2011

Judy Laval Morton
Indiana Starburst,
Year Unknown

BACK COVER
Rita Verroca
Lady of the Lake, 2005

Pat Connally
Lonestar Blues, 2004

Sharon Schamber
Spirit of Mother Earth, 2008

SPINE
Sharon Schamber
Spirit of Mother Earth, 2008

TITLE PAGE
Nancy L. Bardach
Oh! Rock'a My Soul!, 2008

OPPOSITE TITLE PAGE
Marilyn Ward Mowry
Triple Four Patch, 2007

OPPOSITE
Mickey Beebe
Sunflowers & Sawblades,
2003

LARK
An Imprint of Sterling Publishing
387 Park Avenue South
New York, NY 10016

© 2014 by Lark

ISBN 978-1-60059-688-9

Library of Congress Cataloging-in-Publication Data

500 traditional quilts / Karey Bresenhan, Juror.
     pages cm
  ISBN 978-1-60059-688-9
  1. Quilts—History—21st century. I. Bresenhan, Karey, 1942- writer of
supplementary textual content. II. Title: Five hundred traditional quilts.
  NK9110.5.A15 2014
  746.4609'051—dc23

Distributed in Canada by Sterling Publishing
c/o Canadian Manda Group, 165 Dufferin Street
Toronto, Ontario, Canada M6K 3H6
Distributed in the United Kingdom by GMC Distribution Services
Castle Place, 166 High Street, Lewes, East Sussex, England BN7 1XU
Distributed in Australia by Capricorn Link (Australia) Pty. Ltd.
P.O. Box 704, Windsor, NSW 2756, Australia

For information about custom editions, special sales, and premium and corporate purchases, please contact Sterling Special Sales at 800-805-5489 or specialsales@sterlingpublishing.com.

Email academic@larkbooks.com for information about desk and examination copies. The complete policy can be found at larkcrafts.com.

Every effort has been made to ensure that all the information in this book is accurate. However, due to differing conditions, tools, and individual skills, the publisher cannot be responsible for any injuries, losses, and other damages that may result from the use of the information in this book.

Manufactured in China

2 4 6 8 10 9 7 5 3 1

larkcrafts.com

contents

6   Introduction by
     Karey Patterson Bresenhan, Juror

9   The Quilts

426 Contributing Artists

430 Additional Credits

432 About the Juror

432 Acknowledgments

introduction

Traditional quilts will always have a place in people's hearts. Their beauty, their workmanship, their ability to evoke gentler times, the memories they bring to mind—these are integral to their tremendous appeal. In 1995, Jinny Beyer, one of America's consummate traditional quilt artists, spoke to a large audience as she accepted that year's Silver Star Award given by the International Quilt Festival. She brought the room to its feet with her heartfelt statement: "There will always be a place for traditional quilts!" Now, almost 20 years later, Jinny's statement rings as true as ever, and this book is proof of that.

These quilts are the crème de la crème of traditional quiltmaking today. Jurying them was challenging, and while I approached the challenge with eagerness, months later I turned in my selections with reluctance and even a bit of sadness. Why? Because it was so incredibly difficult to make these choices! So many of the quilts that are not in this book could easily have been included...except that the title of the book itself—*500 Traditional Quilts*—set my limit.

But oh, the ones that you will see in these pages! They are spectacular and even awe-inspiring. Some of the designs will be familiar to you; others you may have to study to determine the traditional aspects of the work when your eye may be overwhelmed with its combination of patterns. But the traditional base is always there.

What should you look for? You will see an unusual number of quilts with black and dark backgrounds. You will spot many quilts with acute angles and points sharp enough to delight any lover of precision piecing. You will find many album quilts—wonderful Baltimores, yes, but many other types of unusual, almost idiosyncratic, albums and an assortment of medallion quilts that will appeal to anyone who loves their early counterparts. You will recognize reproduction quilts that are as close to exact copies of nineteenth-century quilts as possible. And on the other hand, you'll see quilts that derive great appeal from their simplicity and clean lines, along with an assortment of charming folk art quilts that are timeless.

There are Log Cabins, surely one of the most traditional of patterns, that you will have to study closely just to discover the pattern itself, and Double Wedding Rings, another beloved pattern, that are transformed with color and embellishment. You'll find alphabet quilts that make you smile and sometimes frown as you search for the letters themselves; miniature quilts that seem impossibly small; Amish quilts taken to a new level with color and fabric choices; wholecloth quilts where the quilting and often the trapunto create masterpieces of remarkable vision and artistry—these are all featured.

You'll note the use of reproduction fabrics, hand-dyed fabrics, commercial fabrics that mimic the look of the hand-dyed originals, batiks, and non-traditional fabrics with texture and sheen. Every color in the rainbow—and many

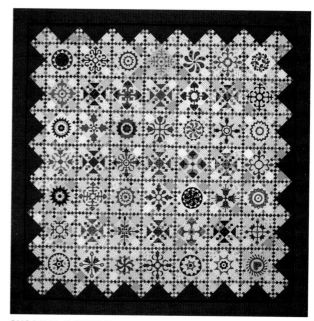

SUSAN H. GARMAN
Afternoon Delight ■ 2012

never seen in any rainbow known to man!—can be found in these stunning quilts. They range from the subtlety of the grey and taupe quilts—often created in Japan—to the air-brushed fantasies and lush coloration of Hawaiian pieces. Exquisite single color quilts are raised to the extraordinary by their elaborate quilting, sometimes by hand, sometimes by machine. Two-color quilts abound, from the stunning blue and white pieces created by Hungarian quilters to redwork quilts. The quilts in this book truly sing with color!

Questions may arise about why certain quilts were selected and others regrettably were not included. Requirements for the book did not specify that an entry had to be an original design, since for centuries, traditional quilts have been made from patterns and rarely have they been original to that quiltmaker. So the use of a pattern did not play a role in the

JOAN DORSAY
Never Again...Again ■ 2009-2011

selection of the quilts. Directions to entrants also did not put a time limit on the quilts, so that a quilt finished 20 years ago had just as much chance of selection as one finished on the day of the deadline. The quilt artist's identity was not revealed so the selection process could be "blind."

There were also photography issues. Although professional photography was not required for entry, the quality of some of the images created a handicap. I would urge quiltmakers who submit quilts for books or shows where the initial decision is based on a photographic image to pay close attention to the quality of their image. For best results, hang or place the quilt vertically (not horizontally) and make sure the image is in sharp focus, lit evenly so the colors are true, with no fingers or feet showing. Shoot outside on an overcast day, and place the quilt against a plain background (such as a garage door). What a shame to lose a marvelous quilt for a book or contest because of photography!

I was fortunate to have the invaluable assistance of Vicki Mangum on the organization and final selection of the images for this book. Vicki, formerly in charge of special exhibits for the Festival in Houston and now involved with exhibits at the Texas Quilt Museum, especially loves traditional quilts, and her first-hand knowledge of the techniques and processes used was a significant help. Her modesty was also remarkable—she never told me she had entered pieces for the book, and it wasn't until we had the final list of the quiltmakers' names that I discovered her work would be represented.

I, too, believe that there will always be a place for traditional quilts. The stunning quilts in this book will speak to people's imaginations, to their fascination with art, to their love of color, to their respect for history, and to their admiration for those who can build on history. They will speak to people's hearts.

—Karey Patterson Bresenhan
President and CEO, Quilts, Inc.
Founder and Director Emeritus, International Quilt Festival

the quilts

Row 1: left **JANET ATKINS**
Kaaterskin ■ 2007–2009
Row 1: center **SACHIKO YOSHIDA**
Nadeshiko - Mother's Beloved Flowers ■ 2010
Row 1: right **KIM MCLEAN**
Roseville Album ■ 2009–2010
Row 2: left **PATRICIA L. DELANEY**
Inspiration Draws from Nature's Art ■ 2008
Row 2: center **LINDA M. ROY**
Wistful Willow ■ 2008
Row 2: right **DEBBY TRACY WALTERS**
Bright Nights ■ 2012

YUYIKO HIRANO
Baltimore Album IV ■ 2004
82 x 82 inches (208.3 x 208.3 cm)
Cotton fabric, batting; hand
appliquéd, pieced and quilted
PHOTO BY MIKE MCCORMIC

FACING PAGE **NORIKO KIDO**
The Endless World II ■ 2008
90 x 72 inches (228.6 x 182.9 cm)
Cotton fabric, cotton and polyester thread,
polyester batting; hand quilted, pieced
PHOTO BY AKINORI MIYASHITA

11

LAURA NOWNES
Harajuku Star ■ 2012
51 x 51 inches (129.5 x 129.5 cm)
Cotton fabrics; machine pieced, raw-edge
fusible appliquéd, machine quilted
QUILTED BY MARLA MONSON
PHOTO BY C+T PUBLISHING CO.

LINDA STEELE
Scottish Dance ■ 2006
72 x 72 inches (182.9 x 182.9 cm)
Cotton fabric, silk thread, wool/polyester batting;
machine quilted, trapunto, hand appliquéd
PHOTO BY ARTIST

13

RITA VERROCA
Lady of the Lake ■ 2005
105 x 105 inches (266.7 x 266.7 cm)
Cotton fabric, cotton thread, cotton batting;
hand appliquéd, hand quilted, hand pieced
PHOTO BY STEVIE VERROCA

KATHLEEN HOLLAND MCCRADY

6 x 6 Comes Up Roses ▪ 1990

101 x 87 inches (256.5 x 221 cm)
Cotton fabric, polyester batting; hand
pieced, hand appliquéd, hand quilted
PHOTO BY JIM & JUDY LINCOLN

SHARON SCHAMBER

Mystique ■ 2010

102 x 102 inches (259.1 x 259.1 cm)
Hand-dyed cotton fabric, silk thread, wool batting; machine
appliquéd, machine pieced, trapunto, corded, bound

PHOTO BY GENE SCHAMBER

500
traditional quilts

HELEN REMICK
Spinning Out Spinning In 4: Rose of Sharon ■ 2007
70 x 74 inches (177.8 x 188 cm)
Cotton fabric, cotton thread, cotton batting; machine quilted, hand appliquéd, machine and hand pieced, paper pieced, hand couched
PHOTOS BY MARK FREY

PAM HILL
Counterpoint ■ 2010
40 x 40 inches (101.6 x 101.6 cm)
Cotton fabric, cotton thread, cotton batting, silk thread, ink, pigment powder; machine quilted, colored
PHOTO BY JULIEN STAR

17

SUNNY EVERETT

Dear Jane ■ 2007

83 x 83 inches (210.8 x 210.8 cm)
Cotton fabric, cotton thread, cotton batting;
hand quilted, hand appliquéd, machine pieced

PHOTO BY TOM KESSLER

SUSAN DAGUE
Food Quilt ■ 1997
84 x 78½ inches (213.4 x 199.4 cm)
Vintage cotton fabric and tea towels, cotton batting,
cotton thread; machine pieced and quilted
PHOTO BY SIBILA SAVAGE

19

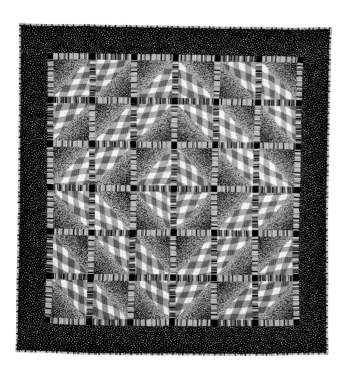

JANE SASSAMAN
Barn Dance ■ 2005
50 x 50 inches (127 x 127 cm)
Cotton fabric, cotton batting; long-
arm machine quilted, pieced
QUILTED BY RISÉ LEVINE
PHOTO BY GREGORY GANTNER

JEAN M. JUDD
Wyoming Valley #5 ■ 2012
97 x 97 inches (246.6 x 246.4 cm)
Cotton fabric, cotton thread, polyester
batting; hand quilted, machine pieced
PHOTO BY ARTIST

JUDITH THOMPSON
Rosy Garden Patch ■ 2005

66½ x 66½ inches (168.9 x 168.9 cm)
Cotton fabric, cotton thread, batting; hand
pieced, hand appliquéd, hand quilted
PHOTO BY RON FARINA PHOTOGRAPHY

21

JANET HAYDAY
Pinwheel Splash ■ 2008
92 x 82 inches (233.7 x 208.3 cm)
Cotton fabrics, thread, and batting; machine quilted
QUILTED BY ANNE HUTCHINSON
PHOTO BY TERON ANSCOMBE

KIM MCLEAN
Basket Medallion ■ 2007
86 x 86 inches (218.4 x 218.4 cm)
Cotton; hand appliquéd and pieced, machine quilted
QUILTED BY KAY FERNIHOUGH
PHOTO BY TIM CONNOLLY

23

SHARI L. STONE
Tropical Bliss ■ 2012

84 x 96 inches (213.4 x 243.8 cm)
Batik fabric, cotton/polyester thread, 80/20 cotton/polyester batting;
machine quilted, machine turn-edge appliquéd, paper pieced
QUILTED BY VICKI RUSSELL, KIT BY JUDY NEIMEYER
PHOTO BY CHERI BLOCKER

TOMPKINS COUNTY QUILTERS GUILD
New York Clambake ■ 2012
87½ x 88½ inches (222.3 x 224.8 cm)
Commercial cotton batik and hand-dyed fabric, cotton thread, cotton batting;
long-arm machine quilted, paper foundation pieced, hand appliquéd
DESIGN BY RUTH A. WHITE, QUILTED BY DEBBIE SANFORD
PHOTO BY ANDREW GILLIS

SUZANNE MARSHALL
Vases ■ 2009
81 x 69½ inches (205.7 x 176.5 cm)
Cotton fabric, polyester batting, embroidery
thread; hand quilted, hand appliquéd
PHOTO BY GARLAND MARSHALL

KEIKO MIYAUCHI
A Rose Garden in a Blue Fence ■ 2007
80³/₄ x 81¹/₂ inches (205.1 x 207 cm)
Cotton fabric, polyester thread, polyester
batting; hand quilted, hand appliquéd, trapunto
PHOTO BY AKINORI MIYASHITA

MEGUMI YOKOYAMA
Crystal in Blue ■ 2007
83 ¾ x 76 ¾ inches (212.7 x 194.9 cm)
Cotton fabric, polyester thread, polyester batting; hand
quilted, hand appliquéd, hand and machine pieced
PHOTO BY MASATO YOKOYAMA

29

RITA VERROCA
The Big Parade ▪ 2004
97 x 97 inches (246.4 x 246.4 cm)
Cotton fabric, cotton thread, cotton batting; hand appliquéd,
hand quilted, hand pieced
PHOTO BY STEVIE VERROCA

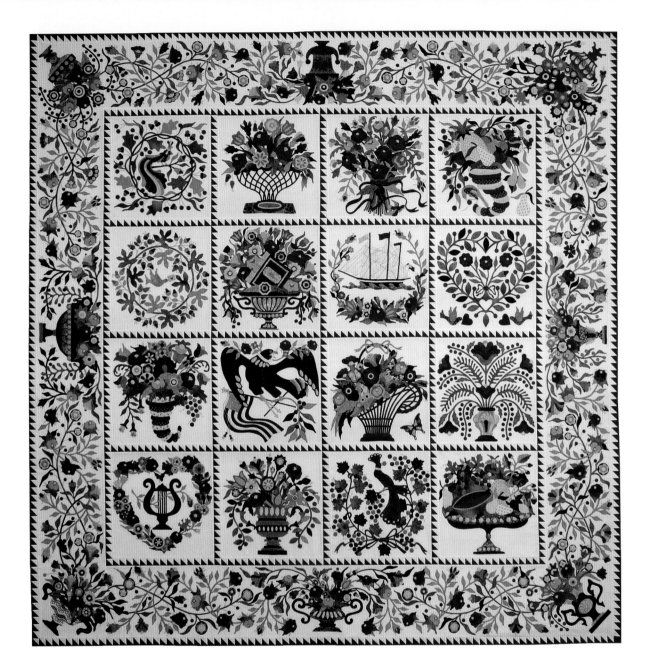

SUSAN H. GARMAN
Friends of Baltimore ■ 2010

87 x 87 inches (221 x 221 cm)
Cotton fabric, cotton thread, wool batting;
hand quilted, appliquéd, pieced
PHOTO BY ARTIST

CAROLE J. DUNKLAU
Aztec (Princess Feathers) ▪ 1998
78 x 78 inches (198.1 x 198.1 cm)
Cotton fabric, cotton thread, polyester batting;
hand appliquéd, machine pieced, machine quilted
QUILTED BY GAYLA BURGER
PHOTO BY ARTIST

CRISTINA SAKA
Shiny Roses (Based on Kathy Nakajima Project) ■ 2011
39 3/8 x 39 3/8 inches (100 x 100 cm)
Hand appliquéd, hand pieced, hand quilted, hand embroidered
PHOTO BY MEIRE MARQUES

SUNNY EVERETT
Cotton Boll Quilt ■ 2006
75 x 75 inches (190.5 x 190.5 cm)
Cotton fabric, cotton thread, cotton batting;
hand quilted, hand appliquéd, machine pieced
PHOTO BY TOM KESSLER

NANCY ELLEN KERNS
Mary Simon Rediscovered ▪ 2004–2010
108 x 108 inches (274.3 x 274.3 cm)
Cotton fabric, silk appliqué thread, polyester batting,
cotton quilting thread; hand appliquéd, hand quilted
PHOTO BY INTERNATIONAL QUILT ASSOCIATION

SUDHA TRIVEDI
Little Brown Bird ▪ 2010
86½ x 86 inches (219.7 x 218.4 cm)
Cotton thread, cotton batting; machine quilted, hand
appliquéd, reverse appliquéd, stuffed appliqué, painted
QUILTED BY MARY JOE YACKLEY
PHOTO BY JIM & JUDY LINCOLN

500
traditional quilts

BEVERLEY REBELO
Yellow Yellow ■ 2010

69 x 69 inches (175.3 x 175.3 cm)
Cotton fabric, cotton thread, bamboo batting;
hand appliquéd, machine pieced, machine quilted
PHOTO BY ARTIST

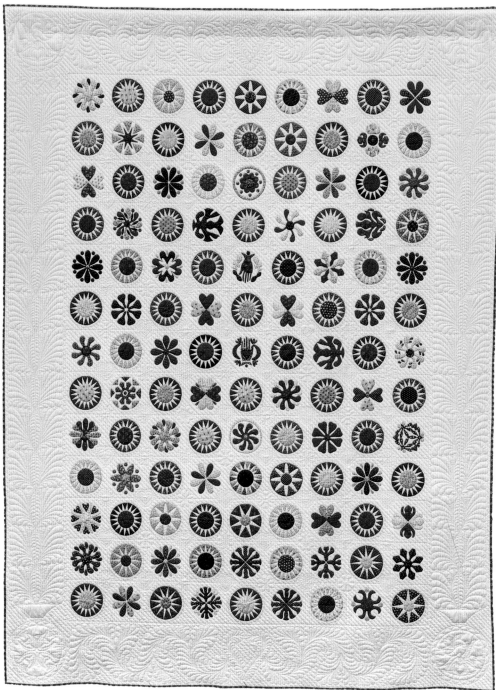

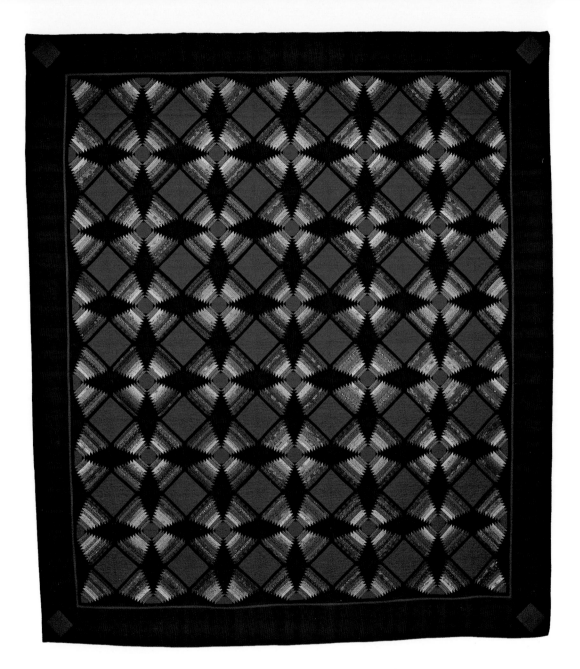

FACING PAGE **KELLEY CUNNINGHAM**
Pennsylvania Hearts and Hands ■ 2011
Cotton fabric, cotton thread, wool batting; hand
appliquéd, paper pieced, machine quilted
PHOTO BY ARTIST

JANE HALL
The Ultimate Pineapple ■ 1997
87 x 76 inches (221 x 193 cm)
Cotton fabric, cotton thread, cotton batting;
machine pieced, hand and machine quilted
PHOTO BY RICHARD COX

37

SUSAN H. GARMAN
Sarah's Revival ■ 2011
88½ x 88½ inches (224.8 x 224.8 cm)
Cotton fabric, cotton thread, wool batting;
hand quilted, appliquéd, pieced
PHOTO BY ARTIST

MARILYN WARD MOWRY
Burgoyne Surrounded in Red – for Wayne ■ 2010
88 x 66 inches (223.5 x 167.6 cm)
Cotton reproduction fabrics, cotton thread, cotton
batting; machine pieced, machine quilted
QUILTED BY SHERI MECOM
PHOTO BY ARTIST

MARGARET MCDONALD
Exuberance ■ 2007

80 x 79½ inches (203.2 x 201.9 cm)
Cotton fabric, cotton thread, cotton batting;
long-arm machine quilted, appliquéd, pieced
QUILTED BY SUSAN CAMPBELL
PHOTO BY J. CHRIS MCDONALD

39

IRENE MCGUIRE ANDREWS
New York Beauty ■ 2011
78 x 75 inches (198.1 x 190.5 cm)
Cotton fabric, cotton thread, cotton batting; machine quilted, paper pieced
QUILTED BY BECKY STOWERS
PHOTO BY STEVE SULLIVAN

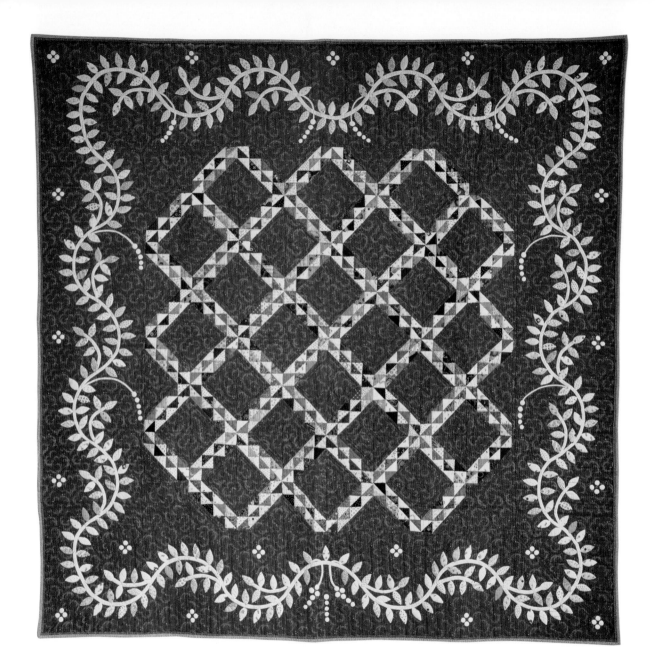

JENNY BACON
The Shirtmaker's Vine ■ 2009

55 x 55 inches (139.7 x 139.7 cm)
Cotton fabric, cotton thread, polyester batting;
hand appliquéd, machine pieced, hand quilted
PHOTO BY CHRIS MCDONALD

41

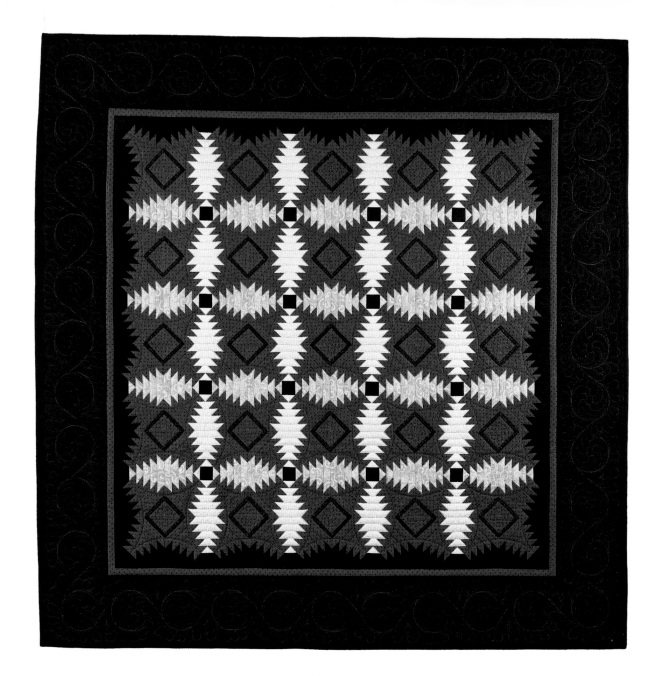

PAT MURPHY HARRISON
Pineapple Patience ■ 2010
41 x 41 inches (104.1 x 104.1 cm)
Cotton fabric, polyester thread, cotton/polyester
blend batting; long-arm machine quilted
PHOTO BY ARTIST

500
traditional quilts

JERRIANNE EVANS
Southern Beauty ■ 2011

72 x 72 inches (182.9 x 182.9 cm)
Cotton fabric, cotton batting; paper pieced, machine pieced, hand appliquéd, machine quilted
QUILTED BY SUE GARMAN, PATTERN BY SUE GARMAN
PHOTO BY JAMES EVANS

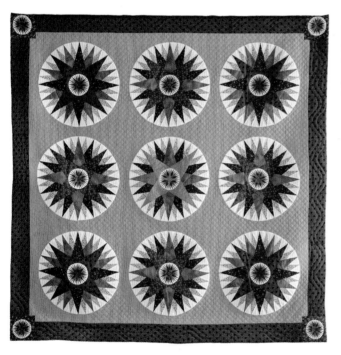

CECILE LACOSTE
Marine Geometry ■ 2009
68 x 68 inches (172.7 x 172.7 cm)
Cotton fabric, cotton thread, cotton batting;
hand appliquéd, hand pieced
PHOTO BY FRANCE PATCHWORK

NANCY A. KING
Scraps at Play ■ 2001
70½ x 53½ inches (179.1 x 135.9 cm)
Cotton fabric, cotton thread, cotton
batting; machine quilted, pieced
PHOTO BY CHRIS FRAWLEY

MARIE-JOSEPHE VETEAU
Upside Down ■ 2009
72 x 72 inches (182.9 x 182.9 cm)
Cotton fabric, cotton thread, cotton batting; hand pieced
PHOTO BY FRANCE PATCHWORK

45

NANCY C. ARSENEAULT
An Unexpected Pleasure ■ 2011

70 x 70 inches (177.8 x 177.8 cm)
Cotton fabrics, cotton and silk threads, wool batting;
machine pieced, machine appliquéd, machine quilted
PHOTO BY INTERNATIONAL QUILT ASSOCIATION

47

SUNNY EVERETT
Crown of Thorns ■ 2003
104 x 79½ inches (264.2 x 201.9 cm)
Cotton fabric, cotton thread, cotton
batting; hand quilted, machine pieced
PHOTO BY TOM KESSLER

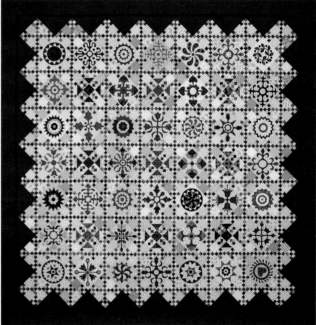

RAMONA BAILEY WILLIAMS
Angel's Puzzle ■ 2002
80 x 66 inches (203.2 x 167.6 cm)
Cotton fabric, cotton thread, cotton batting; machine pieced
QUILTED BY CAROL THELAN
PHOTO BY STILL WATERS PHOTOGRAPHY

SUSAN H. GARMAN
Afternoon Delight ■ 2012
86½ x 86½ inches (219.7 x 219.7 cm)
Cotton fabric, cotton thread, polyester/cotton batting; machine quilted, appliquéd, pieced
PHOTO BY ARTIST

JOAN LEAHY BLANCHARD
Circle of Flowers ■ 2010
88 x 76 inches (223.5 x 193 cm)
Cotton fabric, cotton thread, cotton batting;
machine quilted, hand pieced, appliquéd
QUILTED BY MAUREEN BLANCHARD
PHOTO BY JOANNA KEEFE

LINDA M. ROY
Vintage Button Bouquet ■ 2010
83 x 83 inches (210.8 x 210.8 cm)
Cotton, wool batting; hand appliquéd, hand quilted,
hand embroidered, ruching, machine pieced
PHOTOS BY ARTIST

CYNTHIA COLLIER
Travels In Time ■ 2010

74 x 74 inches (188 x 188 cm)
Cotton fabric, cotton batting;
long-arm quilted, hand appliquéd
QUILTED BY CYNTHIA CLARK
PHOTO BY MIKE MCCORMICK

JANICE L. HEAD
Sun Salutation ■ 2010
42½ x 42½ inches (108 x 108 cm)
Cotton and batik fabric, cotton thread, polyester thread, cotton batting,
monofilament thread, crystals; machine pieced, long-arm machine quilted
PHOTO BY INTERNATIONAL QUILT ASSOCIATION

MARILYN BADGER
Super Star ■ 2011

77 x 77 inches (195.6 x 195.6 cm)
Cotton and silk fabrics, silk thread, cotton batting;
machine pieced, machine appliquéd, machine quilted
PHOTO BY ARTIST

BARBARA A. BLACK
Old Stars, New Day ■ 2011

94 x 94 inches (238.8 x 238.8 cm)
Cotton fabric, cotton thread, wool batting;
machine quilted, machine pieced
QUILTED BY REBECCA MCCARTHY
PHOTO BY JOSHUA BLACK WILKINS

CLAUDIA CLARK MYERS
Casablanca ■ 2005
94 x 94 inches (238.8 x 238.8 cm)
Cotton fabric, rayon thread, 80/20 batting;
long-arm machine quilted, machine pieced
QUILTED BY MARILYN BADGER
PHOTOS BY ARTIST

MARGARET PHILLIPS CURLEY
Follow Me ■ 2006
84 x 84 inches (213.4 x 213.4 cm)
Cotton fabrics, cotton thread, polyester/cotton batting;
hand quilted, machine pieced, hand appliquéd
PHOTO BY PITTSBURGH CUSTOM DARKROOM

SUSAN ATKINSON
Blue Bell Woods ■ 2005
108 x 108 inches (274.3 x 274.3 cm)
Batik fabric, cotton thread, wool batting; hand and
machine quilted, hand appliquéd, machine pieced
PHOTO BY MARGARET HUTCHBY

FACING PAGE **LUDY BALMAT**
Why Not ■ 2008
71 x 58 inches (180.3 x 147.3 cm)
English paper pieced
PHOTO BY GEORGE CHAMBERS JR.

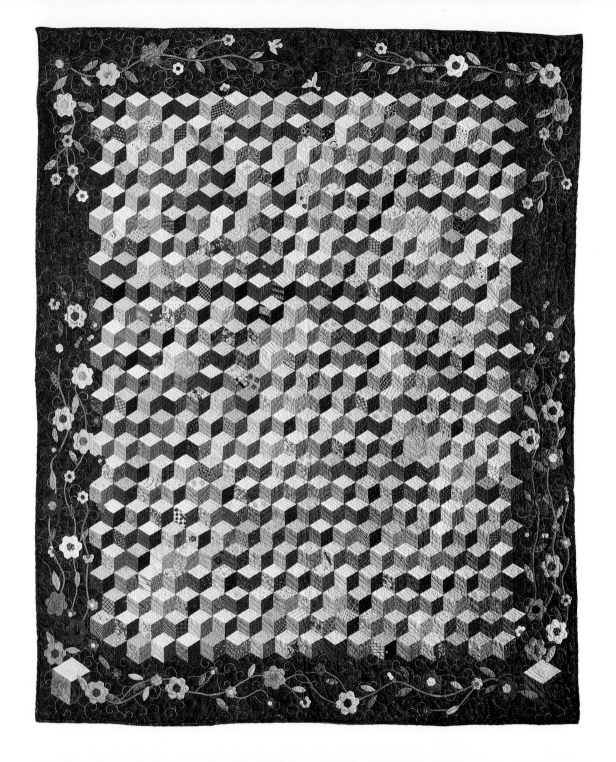

57

GEANNINE OTT

Four & Twenty Blackbirds ■ 2010

59 3/4 x 59 1/4 inches (151.8 x 150.5 cm)
Cotton fabric, cotton thread; machine pieced,
hand appliquéd, machine quilted, trapunto
QUILTED BY MARCELLA PICKETT
PHOTO BY ROBERT CHAMBERS

FAYE ANDERSON
Serenity ■ 2011
77 x 77 inches (195.6 x 195.6 cm)
Cotton fabric, cotton thread, cotton batting;
hand quilted, appliquéd, pieced

JANET ATKINS
Kaaterskin ■ 2007–2009
81½ x 81½ inches (207 x 207 cm)
Cotton fabric, cotton thread, polyester batting;
hand pieced, hand appliquéd, hand quilted
PHOTO BY WILMA HART, INTERNATIONAL QUILT ASSOCIATION

ANN L. PETERSEN
Spring in My Step ■ 2009
70 x 70 inches (177.8 x 177.8 cm)
Cotton and silk fabrics, cotton, polyester, nylon, and silk
thread, cotton batting, crystal beads; machine pieced,
machine appliquéd, machine quilted, hand beaded
PHOTOS BY GREGORY CASE PHOTOGRAPHY

KRISTIN VIERRA
Mom's Flower Garden ■ 2010

90 x 90 inches (228.6 x 228.6 cm)
Cotton fabric, cotton thread, polyester thread, cotton and polyester batting;
hand appliquéd, machine pieced, machine quilted
PHOTO BY ARTIST

FACING PAGE **DONNA KNIGHT**
Linda's Musical Garden ■ 2006
53 x 46½ inches (134.6 x 118.1 cm)
Cotton fabric, wool batting; hand quilted, hand
appliquéd, machine pieced, hand embroidered
PHOTO BY JAYDEE'S PHOTOGRAPHY

JANICE MILLER BRADY
Loada Moda Scraps ■ 2004
84 x 86 inches (213.4 x 218.4 cm)
Cotton fabric, cotton thread, wool batting;
hand quilted, hand appliquéd, machine pieced
PHOTO BY JIM & JUDY LINCOLN

LYNN FOLLIS
Leaves and Acorns ■ 2009
100 x 78 inches (254 x 198.1 cm)
QUILTED BY KAREN OVERTON
PHOTO BY MIKE MCCORMICK

JERRIANNE EVANS
Carrie Hall Sampler ■ 2011
84 x 74 inches (213.4 x 188 cm)
Cotton fabric, cotton batting; paper pieced, hand appliquéd, machine pieced, machine quilted
BLOCKS DESIGNED BY BARBARA BRACKMAN, SUE GARMAN, AND ARTIST
QUILTED BY CYNTHIA CLARK
PHOTOS BY JAMES EVANS

JAYNETTE HUFF
Wrought Iron and Roses ■ 2010

95½ x 96 inches (242.6 x 243.8 cm)
Cotton fabric, ultrasuede, cotton/polyester batting; paper foundation
pieced, hand appliquéd, machine appliquéd, machine quilted
PHOTO BY ARTIST

65

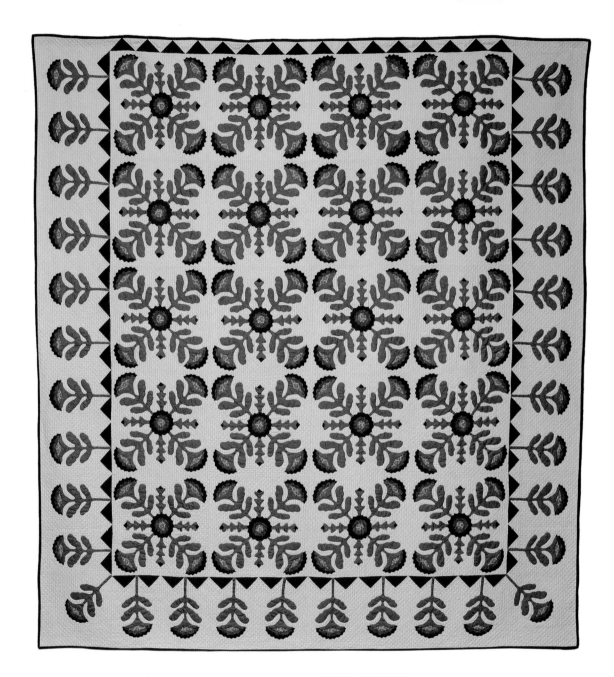

CONNIE WATKINS
Colonial Cockscomb ■ 2006
94½ x 88½ inches (240 x 224.8 cm)
Cotton fabric, cotton thread, wool batting;
hand quilted, hand appliquéd
PHOTO BY ARTIST

MICHELE A. BARNES
Houston County Elegance ■ 2006
83½ x 83½ inches (212.1 x 212.1 cm)
Cotton fabric, cotton thread, cotton batting; hand quilted,
hand appliquéd, machine assembled
PHOTO BY PHIL BARNES

SALLY MAGEE
Brown Bird's Lullaby ■ 2009
85 x 85 inches (215.9 x 215.9 cm)
Cotton fabric, silk batting, cotton and silk
thread; pieced, appliquéd, trapunto, corded,
hand and machine quilted, embroidered

MERRY MAY
Hunter's Star (Big Red) ■ 2009
102 x 88 inches (259.1 x 223.5 cm)
Cotton fabric, cotton thread, cotton batting;
machine pieced, machine quilted
QUILTED BY LINDA J. HAHN

HOLLY SWEET, JANICE BADGER, JENNY COPELAND, LESLIE EMMA, TESS GRIFFIN, JEAN HOUGHTBY, DEIRDRE JERSEY, SUSAN LUMPKIN, JEANNE MCBRAYER, DOROTHY NEMY, KAROL PARHAM, CAROLYN RUBY, MARGARET SLADE, JUNE VOLSTAD

Bittersweet Medallion ■ 2007

64 x 64 inches (162.6 x 162.6 cm)
Cotton fabric, cotton and perle cotton thread, polyester batting;
hand quilted, hand appliquéd, machine pieced
PHOTO BY MAGGIE WILSON

69

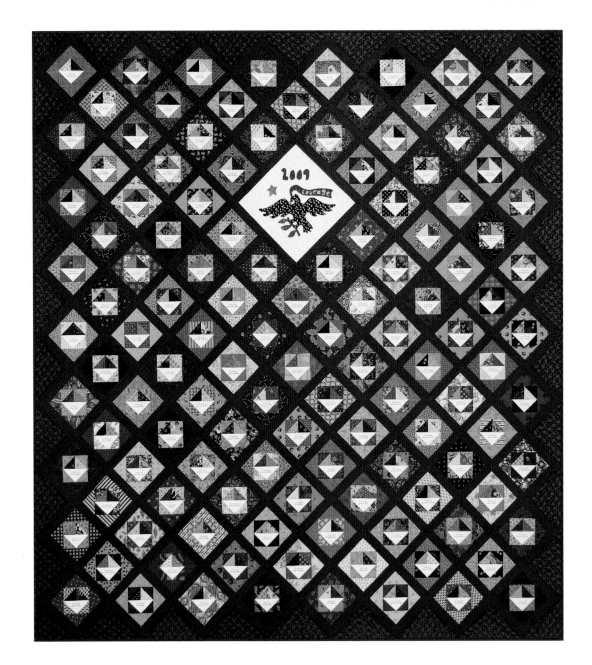

BECKY FULLER STEPHENSON
The Courage Quilt ■ 2009

97 x 86 inches (246.4 x 218.4 cm)
Cotton fabric, cotton thread, cotton batting;
machine pieced, hand appliquéd, machine quilted
APPLIQUÉD BY JERRIANNE EVANS, QUILTED BY SUSAN GARMAN
PHOTO BY JIM EVANS

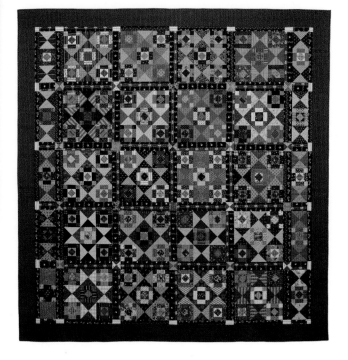

JAN SOULES
Vence Remembered ■ 2010

94 x 73 inches (238.8 x 185.4 cm)
Cotton fabric, cotton thread, 80/20
batting; long-arm quilted, pieced

QUILTED BY DEBBIE LOPEZ
PHOTOS BY RICK RICHARDS

CAROL STAEHLE
Ohio Star ■ 2010

78 x 76 inches (198.1 x 193 cm)
Cotton fabrics; machine pieced, machine quilted

QUILTED BY SHERI MECOM
PHOTO BY ANNETTE PLOG

71

MARGARET MCDONALD
Propelled ■ 2009

93 x 92 inches (236.2 x 233.7 cm)
Cotton fabric, cotton thread, cotton batting; appliquéd, pieced
QUILTED BY SUSAN CAMPBELL
PHOTO BY J. CHRIS MCDONALD

LESLIE KIGER
Logs and Stars in Scraps ■ 2010

84 x 84 inches (213.4 x 213.4 cm)
Cotton fabrics, cotton thread, 80/20 batting; machine pieced
QUILTED BY JOAN KNIGHT
PHOTO BY ARTIST

73

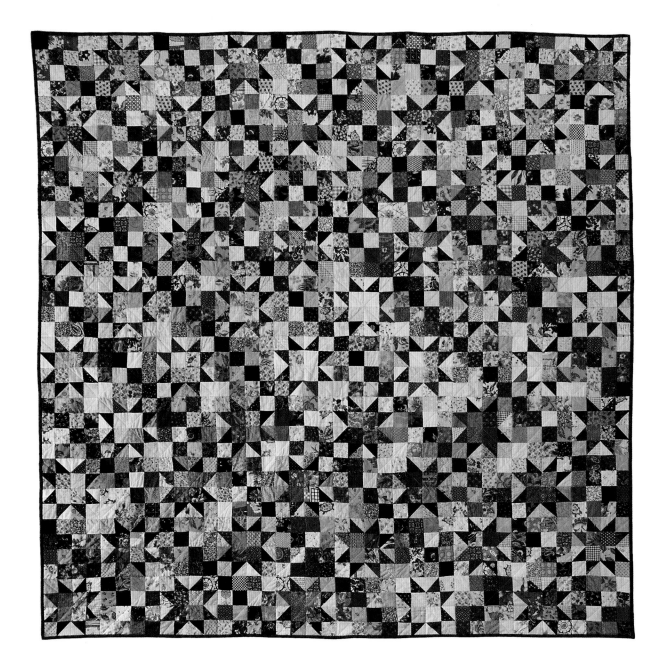

SUSAN DEUPREE JONES
Crossroads Through Connecticut ■ 2012
80 x 80 inches (203.2 x 203.2 cm)
Cotton fabric, cotton/polyester batting and thread;
machine pieced and quilted
PHOTO BY ARTIST

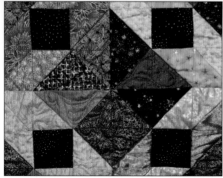

BETH CAMERON
Shining Stars ■ 2009
94 x 81 inches (238.8 x 205.7 cm)
Cotton fabrics with metallic sparkles, cotton thread,
80/20 batting; machine quilted, pieced
PATTERN BY THE RABBIT FACTORY
PHOTOS BY RAY PILON

JEAN M. JUDD
Wyoming Valley #1 (Choir of Angels Tapestry) ■ 2005
81 x 81 inches (205.7 x 205.7 cm)
Cotton fabric, cotton thread, polyester batting;
hand quilted, machine pieced
PHOTO BY ARTIST

PAT KUHNS
Emiline ■ 2009
16½ x 16½ inches (41.9 x 41.9 cm)
Cotton fabric, cotton thread, cotton batting;
machine quilted, hand appliquéd, pieced
PHOTO BY ARTIST

LAREE STOKES
Nebraska's Rising Sun ■ 2009
64 x 64 inches (162.6 x 162.6 cm)
Cotton fabrics; hand appliquéd, machine quilted
PHOTO BY KIT STOKES

BEVERLEY REBELO
African Savanna ■ 2010

64 x 64 inches (162.6 x 162.6 cm)
African cotton fabric, cotton thread, cotton batting, metal,
glass, shell; machine pieced, machine quilted, embellished
PHOTO BY ARTIST

HIROMI YOKOTA
GOOD! YOKOHAMA! I LOVE YOKOHAMA! ■ 2004
71 x 61 inches (180.3 x 154.9 cm)
Cotton fabric, polyester thread, polyester batting;
hand quilted, pieced, hand embroidered
PHOTO BY ARTIST

NANCY S. BROWN
The Niebur Sisters ▨ 2002

46 x 52 inches (116.8 x 132.1 cm)
Cotton fabric, cotton thread, 80/20 batting; hand quilted,
hand appliquéd, machine pieced
PHOTO BY ARTIST

SUSAN WEBB LEE
Color Study ■ 1996
42 x 42 inches (106.7 x 106.7 cm)
Hand-dyed cotton fabric, cotton embroidery floss,
cotton thread, cotton batting; hand pieced
PHOTO BY STEVE MANN

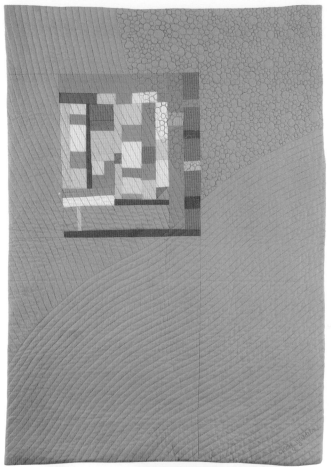

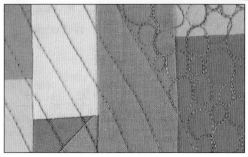

CINDY GRISDELA
Amber Harvest ■ 2009
34 x 24 inches (86.4 x 61 cm)
Cotton batik fabric, cotton variegated thread,
cotton batting; machine quilted, pieced
PHOTOS BY GREGORY STALEY

CHRISTINE WEBB
Broken Dishes from the Colorful World Collection ■ 2010
22¼ x 22¼ inches (56.5 x 56.5 cm)
Cotton fabric, polyester thread, cotton
batting; machine quilted, pieced
PHOTO BY SCOT GORDON

81

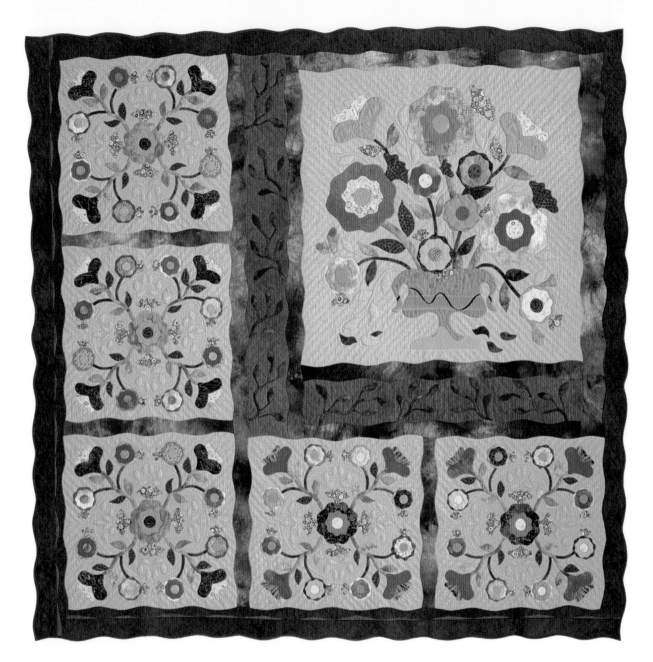

FACING PAGE **MICKEY BEEBE**
Sunflowers & Sawblades ■ 2003

79 x 57 inches (200.7 x 144.8 cm)
Cotton fabric, 80/20 batting; hand-guided
machine quilted, hand appliquéd, pieced
QUILTED BY MARY LUNDBERG
PHOTO BY ALAN PORTER

ANDREA PEREJDA
Whigged Out on the West Coast ■ 2001

75 x 75 inches (190.5 x 190.5 cm)
Cotton sateen, hand-dyed cotton fabrics, cotton thread, cotton
batting; hand appliquéd, hand quilted, padded, cord work
PHOTO BY ALAN EDELMAN

CHRISTINE N. BROWN
Petals ■ 1998
50 x 55½ inches (127 x 141 cm)
Hand-dyed and commercial cotton fabrics, cotton thread,
cotton batting; hand quilted, hand appliquéd, machine pieced
PHOTO BY ARTIST

BEVERLEY REBELO
Fab Quilt ■ 2011
65½ x 53 inches (166.4 x 134.6 cm)
Cotton fabric, invisible thread, cotton thread,
cotton batting; machine pieced and quilted
PHOTO BY ARTIST

MERELYN JAYNE PEARCE
Gymea and Waratahs ■ 2009
57 x 46½ inches (144.8 x 118.1 cm)
Cotton fabrics, cotton thread, monofilament thread,
polyester batting; hand appliquéd, hand embroidered,
trapunto, machine quilted
PHOTO BY UNKNOWN

85

HAZEL CANNY
Vase of Flowers ■ 2001
97 x 77 inches (246.4 x 195.6 cm)
Cotton sateen fabric, cotton thread,
batting; hand quilted, hand appliquéd

VICKI COODY MANGUM
Nancy's Glorious Flower Basket ■ 1994
54 x 45 inches (137.2 x 114.3 cm)
Cotton and silk fabrics, hand-dyed fabrics, cotton and
embroidery threads, cotton/polyester batting; hand appliquéd,
hand quilted, hand embroidered, machine quilted

KEIKO MIYAUCHI
A Bouquet of Yellow Roses ■ 2004
83 3/4 x 83 3/4 inches (212.7 x 212.7 cm)
Cotton fabric, polyester thread, polyester batting;
hand quilted, hand appliquéd, trapunto

SANDRA L. MOLLON
Baltimore Album Medallion ■ 2002–2009

100 x 100 inches (254 x 254 cm)
Cotton and silk fabrics, silk and cotton thread, silk batting;
machine quilted, hand appliquéd, machine pieced
QUILTED BY CREATIVE QUILTS OF GALT, CA
PHOTO BY ARTIST

GEORGINA BUSCHAUER
Challenge 2 ■ 2011
82¼ x 82¼ inches (208.9 x 208.9 cm)
Cotton fabric, cotton thread, wool batting; hand quilted,
hand appliquéd, machine pieced, trapunto
PHOTOS BY MIKE MCCORMICK

MARGARET PHILLIPS CURLEY
Album From Pittsburgh ■ 2003
76 x 76 inches (193 x 193 cm)
Cotton fabric, cotton thread, polyester/cotton
batting; hand quilted, hand appliquéd
BLOCKS BY JANE TOWNSWICK
PHOTO BY PITTSBURGH CUSTOM DARKROOM

89

BETTY NEW
Venus DiVine ▦ 2012
46 x 45½ inches (116.8 x 115.6 cm)
Cotton fabric, cotton threads, wool batting; machine appliquéd,
machine pieced, hand-guided free-motion quilted, embellished
PHOTO BY ICONIK STUDIOS

NAOKO HAYASHI
Campanula ■ 2011
83 x 75 inches (210.8 x 190.5 cm)
Cotton fabric; hand quilted, appliquéd
PHOTO BY TOSHIKATSU WATANABE

LOUISE-MARIE STIPON
Botanical Page ■ 2009
88 9/16 x 88 9/16 inches (225 x 225 cm)
Cotton fabric, cotton thread, cotton batting; hand appliquéd
PHOTO BY FRANCE PATCHWORK

HILARY GOODING
YOLANDE MACHEMER

Sleeping Beauty ■ 2005

96 x 96 inches (243.8 x 243.8 cm)
Cotton fabric, cotton and rayon thread, polyester/cotton batting;
machine quilted, appliquéd, pieced
QUILTED BY TRACEY PEREIRA
PHOTO BY KEVIN MEAD

93

KRISTIN VIERRA
Flowers & Feathers ■ 2012
70 x 74 inches (177.8 x 188 cm)
Cotton fabric, polyester thread, cotton batting;
trapunto, machine quilted
PHOTOS BY ARTIST

PAM HILL
Peppermint Twist ■ 2011
40 x 40 inches (101.6 x 101.6 cm)
Hand-dyed cotton fabric, cotton and wool
batting, silk thread; machine quilted
PHOTO BY JULIEN STAR

RACHELLE DENNENY
Golden Ivory ■ 2012
91 x 88½ inches (231.1 x 224.8 cm)
Cotton sateen fabric, wool batting, metallic and polyester threads;
free-motion embroidered, trapunto, machine quilted
PHOTO BY JIM & JUDY LINCOLN

KATHY MCNEIL
GERI PARKER
Feathered Friends ■ 2008
71½ x 71½ inches (181.6 x 181.6 cm)
Hand appliquéd, machine paper pieced,
trapunto, hand and machine embroidered
PHOTO BY BRUCE MCNEIL

KATHY K. WYLIE

Instruments of Praise ■ 2009

68 1/2 x 68 1/2 inches (174 x 174 cm)
Cotton and silk fabrics, cotton and nylon threads, wool and cotton/polyester blend battings;
hand appliquéd, hand embroidered, hand couched threads and cord, domestic machine quilted
COLLECTION OF THE NATIONAL QUILT MUSEUM OF THE UNITED STATES
PHOTO BY ALEX ROBERTSON

JUDITH THOMPSON
Vines and Baskets ■ 2004–2005

78 x 78 inches (198.1 x 198.1 cm)
Cotton fabric, cotton thread, batting;
hand pieced, hand appliquéd, hand quilted
PHOTO BY RON FARINA PHOTOGRAPHY

SUSAN STEWART
TulipFire ■ 2012

70 x 70 inches (177.8 x 177.8 cm)
Cotton and silk fabric, cotton and polyester thread, cotton batting;
machine pieced, machine embroidered, shaped lace insertion,
pintucked, machine stitched, free-motion machine quilted
PHOTO BY ARTIST

MONNA KORNMAN
Variations on Jacobean ■ 1996
107 x 88 inches (271.8 x 223.5 cm)
Cotton fabric, cotton thread, cotton batting;
hand quilted, appliquéd, machine pieced
PHOTO BY JIM & JUDY LINCOLN

KEIKO MIYAUCHI
Tree of Life ■ 2009
80¼ x 81 inches (203.8 x 205.7 cm)
Cotton fabric, polyester thread, polyester batting;
hand quilted, hand appliquéd, trapunto
PHOTO BY AKINORI MIYASHITA

101

CYNTHIA COLLIER
Audubon in Appliqué ■ 2012
76 x 76 inches (193 x 193 cm)
Cotton fabric, cotton batting; long-arm quilted,
hand appliquéd
QUILTED BY DENISE GREEN
PHOTO BY MIKE MCCORMICK

BARBARA KORENGOLD
Lost Boy ■ 2006–2007
81 x 70½ inches (205.7 x 179.1 cm)
Cotton and silk fabrics, cotton and silk threads, wool batting;
hand appliquéd, hand embroidered, hand quilted,
machine pieced
PHOTO BY PAUL ELBO

JANICE VAINE
Garden Rhapsody ■ 2010

64 x 64 inches (162.6 x 162.6 cm)
Cotton fabric, silk, ultra suede, cotton and silk threads, silk ribbon, ombre wired ribbon, beads, wool batting; hand appliquéd, silk ribbon embroidery, hand embroidered, ribbonwork, stumpwork

QUILTED BY MARILYN LANGE
STITCHED BY JO ANN CRIDGE, DORIS DOWLING, LUELLA M. DUSEK, SANDY AMADOR DUSEK, GENA HOLLAND, CAROLYN GOFF
KIMBLE, MELISSA S. MATTZ, RUTHE TOTH, MARY T. TOZER, JAN VAINE, MARA WARWICK, RONDA GEISLER WOODS
COURTESY OF LANDAUER PUBLISHING
PHOTO BY SUE VOEGTLIN

FACING PAGE **CAROLE J. DUNKLAU**
Autumn Gatherings ■ 1992
104 x 90 inches (264.2 x 228.6 cm)
Cotton fabric, cotton thread, polyester batting;
hand appliquéd, machine pieced
QUILTED BY CAROL WURTH, DESIGN BY MURIEL DOUGLAS AND PATTY MILLER
PHOTO BY ARTIST

ZENA THORPE
Out of the Strong Came Forth Sweetness ■ 1998
76 x 86 inches (193 x 218.4 cm)
Cotton fabric, cotton thread, cotton batting;
hand quilted, hand appliquéd
PHOTO BY DONALD LEVINE

105

MERELYN JAYNE PEARCE

Preston Dreaming ■ Year Unknown

88 x 92¹/₂ inches (223.5 x 235 cm)
Cotton fabrics, cotton thread, monofilament thread, silk thread,
polyester batting; hand appliquéd, hand embroidered, machine quilted

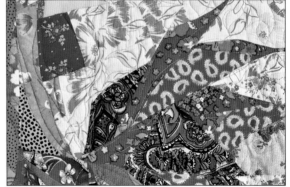

PATRICIA G. FAULKNER
At the Water Trough ■ 2009
48 x 48 inches (121.9 x 121.9 cm)
Hand-painted background, cotton fabric, cotton thread, cotton batting;
hand appliquéd, hand embroidered, hand and machine quilted
PHOTOS BY TERRENCE W. FAULKNER

OLGA MILOVANOVA
Peasant Yard ■ 2006
42 x 43 inches (106.7 x 109.2 cm)
Cotton fabric, cotton thread, cotton
batting; machine quilted, appliquéd
PHOTOS BY ARTIST

107

LINDA STEELE
Naturally Crazy ■ 2012
67 x 67 inches (170.2 x 170.2 cm)
Cotton fabric, cotton and silk thread, wool/polyester batting;
machine quilted, hand embroidered, hand beaded
PHOTO BY ARTIST

KIM MCLEAN
Pandemonium Quilt ■ 2011

92 x 92 inches (233.7 x 233.7 cm)
Cotton; hand appliquéd and pieced, machine quilted
QUILTED BY KAY FERNIHOUGH
PHOTO BY TIM CONNOLLY

JENNY CHIOVARO
Kaffe and Karen Take Sue to New York ■ 2012
55 x 48 inches (139.7 x 121.9 cm)
Cotton fabric, silk and polyester thread, polyester batting;
machine pieced, hand appliquéd, machine quilted
PHOTO BY ARTIST

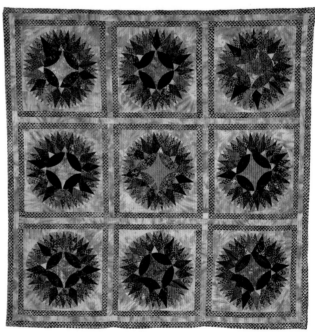

KATHLEEN L. CARLSON
New York Minute ■ 2011
21¼ x 21¼ inches (54 x 54 cm)
Cotton batiks, silk thread, cotton batting; machine embroidered,
machine quilted, hand beaded
PHOTO BY ARTIST

LYNETTE S. JACKSON
Batik Sunflowers ■ 2011
91 x 91 inches (231.1 x 231.1 cm)
Cotton fabric, cotton thread, cotton batting;
hand quilted, appliquéd, pieced
PHOTO BY JULIE YARBROUGH

MARILYN BADGER
Bali Hai ■ 2009
95 x 95 inches (241.3 x 241.3 cm)
Cotton and silk fabrics, metallic thread, cotton batting;
machine pieced, machine appliquéd, machine quilted
DESIGNED BY CLAUDIA CLARK MYERS
PHOTO BY ARTIST

FACING PAGE **ALICE FUCHS GARRARD**
Rally Round Raspberry Ruff ■ 1999
114 x 77 inches (289.6 x 195.6 cm)
Cotton fabric, rayon and cotton thread, wool
batting; machine quilted, machine pieced
PHOTO BY MELLISA KARLIN MAHONEY
FOR QUILTERS NEWSLETTER

JUDITH THOMPSON
Feathers Aglow ■ 2009
71 x 71 inches (180.3 x 180.3 cm)
Cotton fabric, cotton thread, batting; hand pieced,
hand appliquéd, hand quilted
PHOTO BY RON FARINA PHOTOGRAPHY

SUSAN STEWART
GLORIA MEYER
Gloria's Garden ■ 2009
73 x 73 inches (185.4 x 185.4 cm)
Cotton fabric, cotton and polyester thread, cotton
batting; embroidered, free-motion machine quilted
PHOTOS BY ARTISTS

LORI SCHMITT ALLISON
Lone Star ■ 2012
52 x 52 inches (132.1 x 132.1 cm)
Cotton fabric, cotton thread, cotton
batting; hand pieced, hand quilted
PHOTO BY GREGORY CASE PHOTOGRAPHY

MARY KAY DAVIS
Sweet Scents at Sunrise ■ 2009
60 x 60 inches (152.4 x 152.4 cm)
Cotton fabric, cotton thread, cotton batting; machine quilted, machine appliquéd, machine pieced
PHOTO BY ARTIST

MARGARET PHILLIPS CURLEY
Fancy Feathers ■ 2004
81 x 81 inches (205.7 x 205.7 cm)
Cotton fabrics, cotton thread, polyester/cotton batting; hand quilted, machine pieced, hand appliquéd
PHOTOS BY PITTSBURGH CUSTOM DARKROOM

BARBARA A. BLACK
Joyful Journey ■ 2009

87 x 87 inches (221 x 221 cm)
Cotton fabric, cotton thread, cotton batting; machine quilted, machine pieced
QUILTED BY PAMELA JOY SPENCER DRANSFELDT
PHOTO BY JOSHUA BLACK WILKINS

IRENE MCGUIRE ANDREWS
Bloomin' Log Cabin ■ 2012
96 x 81 inches (243.8 x 205.7 cm)
Cotton fabric, cotton thread, cotton batting; machine pieced, machine appliquéd
QUILTED BY DOT PIKE
PHOTO BY STEVE SULLIVAN

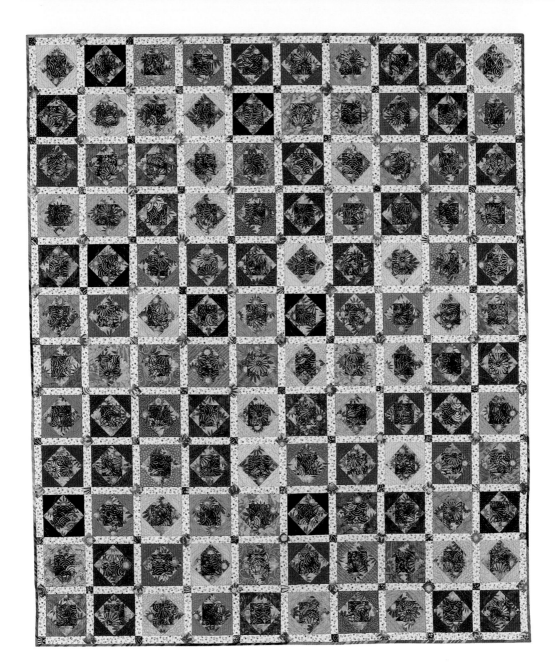

WENDY HILL
Cherry Phosphate ■ 2002
84 x 71 inches (213.4 x 180.3 cm)
Assorted cotton prints, commercial batiks; pieced, machine quilted
PHOTO BY CRAIG HOWELL

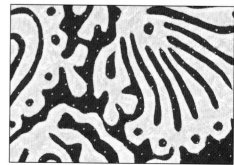

ALICE TIGNOR
Eternal Stars ▥ 2009
12½ x 12½ inches (31.8 x 31.8 cm)
Cotton fabric, cotton thread, cotton batting;
hand quilted, machine pieced
PHOTOS BY JIM & JUDY LINCOLN

MÁRIA MOLNÁR JÁNOSNÉ
Hungarian Motifs from Csorna ▥ 2000
64 x 48 inches (162.6 x 121.9 cm)
Cotton fabric, cotton thread, polyester batting;
hand quilted, appliquéd, pieced
PHOTOS BY LÁSZLÓ JANTNER

DIANE LOOMIS
Blues Sampler ■ 2008

50 x 50 inches (127 x 127 cm)
Cotton fabric, cotton and silk thread, wool batting; machine quilted,
hand and machine pieced
STAR AND PINEAPPLE BLOCK PATTERNS BY JINNY BEYER
PHOTO BY ARTIST

NANCY A. KING
Batik Kaleidoscope ■ 1999
102 x 84 inches (259.1 x 213.4 cm)
Cotton fabric, cotton thread, cotton batting; machine quilted, pieced
PHOTO BY CHRIS FRAWLEY

FRAN SNAY
Twylite Zone ■ 2001

91 x 72 inches (231.1 x 182.9 cm)
Cotton fabric, cotton thread, cotton batting; machine
quilted, machine pieced, needle-turn appliquéd
QUILTED BY LINDA TAYLOR
PHOTO BY INTERNATIONAL QUILT ASSOCIATION

123

MARGARET "PEGGY" FETTERHOFF
Floral Phantasma ■ 1998
96 x 96 inches (243.8 x 243.8 cm)
Cotton fabric, cotton thread, cotton batting; hand quilted, machine pieced
PHOTO BY JIM & JUDY LINCOLN

MEGUMI YOKOYAMA
Twilight Garden ■ 2005

78 3/4 x 78 3/4 inches (200 x 200 cm)
Cotton fabric, polyester thread, polyester batting; hand quilted,
hand appliquéd, hand and machine pieced
PHOTO BY MASATO YOKOYAMA

125

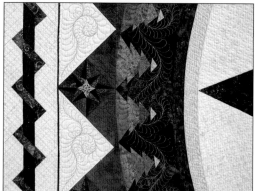

BETTY L. BRISTER
My Friends Made Me Do It, aka Starlight Garden ■ 2010
92 x 92 inches (233.7 x 233.7 cm)
Cotton fabrics, cotton thread, batting; machine
pieced, hand appliquéd and quilted
PHOTOS BY JIM & JUDY LINCOLN

SHERRY REYNOLDS
Christmas All Around ■ 2010

87 x 87 inches (221 x 221 cm)
Cotton fabric, cotton thread, silk thread, polyester thread,
cotton batting, glass beads, crystals; machine quilted,
machine appliquéd, machine pieced, embellished
PHOTOS BY JIM & JUDY LINCOLN

PAT CONNALLY
Lonestar Blues ■ 2004

90 x 90 inches (228.6 x 228.6 cm)
Cotton fabric, cotton thread; machine pieced, long-arm machine quilted

PATTERN BY DERECK LOCKWOOD
PHOTO BY JIM & JUDY LINCOLN

DIANNE FIRTH
Fading Stars ■ 1992
75 x 75 inches (190.5 x 190.5 cm)
Cotton fabric, cotton thread, polyester batting;
hand quilted, machine pieced
PHOTO BY ARTIST

MARIAN ANN MONTGOMERY
Circles of Periwinkle ■ 2010

84 x 84 inches (213.4 x 213.4 cm)
Cotton fabric, cotton thread, wool batting; machine quilted, pieced
QUILTED BY RICHARD LARSON
DESIGN BY IRENE BERRY
PHOTO BY BRAD FLOWERS

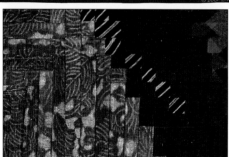

EMIKO TODA LOEB
Amiu (Asian Galaxy) front and back ■ 2001
82¹/₂ x 62 inches (209.6 x 157.5 cm)
Old cotton, cotton thread, cotton batting; pieced, quilted
PHOTOS BY KAREN BELL

ANITA GROSSMAN SOLOMON
Old Italian Block Quilt ■ 2004

76 x 70 inches (193 x 177.8 cm)
Cotton fabric, cotton thread, cotton batting; machine quilted, pieced
QUILTED BY JANICE E. PETRE
PHOTO BY CHRISTINA CARTY-FRANCIS & DIANE PEDERSON

131

500
traditional quilts

FACING PAGE **JANE HALL**
Galaxy ■ 2001

90 x 72 inches (228.6 x 182.9 cm)
Cotton fabric, cotton thread, cotton/polyester batting;
machine pieced, hand and machine quilted
PHOTO BY RICHARD COX

CHRIS SERONG
Feathered Star ■ 2009

67 x 67 inches (170.2 x 170.2 cm)
Cotton fabric, cotton thread, wool batting; hand and
machine pieced, hand and machine quilted
QUILTED BY SUSAN CAMPBELL
PHOTO BY ARTIST

133

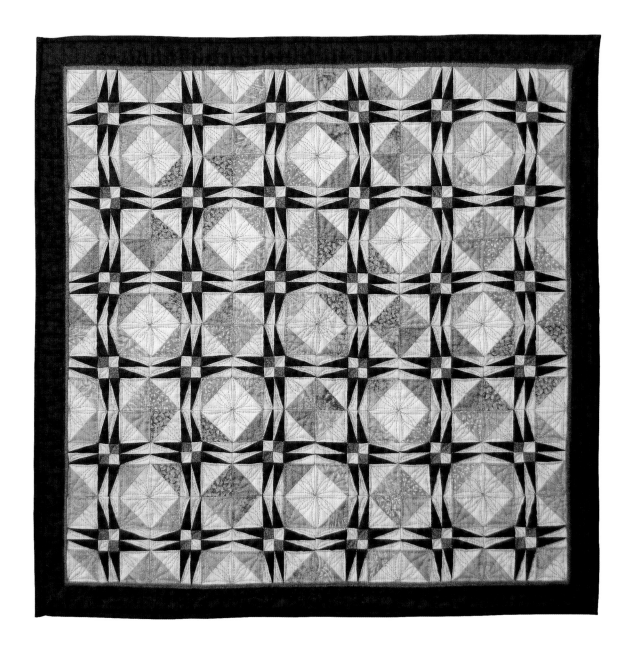

LEIGH ELKING
Laughing Irish Eyes ■ 2004
18 x 18 inches (45.7 x 45.7 cm)
Cotton fabric, cotton and metallic thread, batting;
machine pieced and quilted
PHOTO BY ARTIST

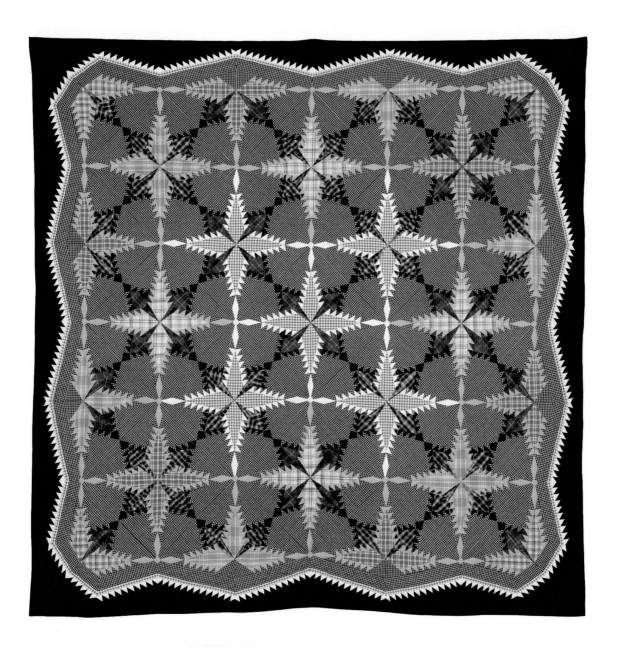

GABRIELLE PAQUIN
Double Feather Star ■ 2009
86 5/8 x 86 5/8 inches (220 x 220 cm)
Cotton fabric, cotton thread, cotton batting; pieced
PHOTO BY FRANCE PATCHWORK

CINDY SEITZ-KRUG
Bluer than Blue ■ 2005
102 x 96 inches (259.1 x 243.8 cm)
Cotton fabrics, 80/20 cotton/polyester batting, rayon and
invisible nylon thread; machine quilted, machine appliquéd
PHOTO BY TOM ALEXANDER

MÁRIA MOLNÁR JÁNOSNÉ
My Flowers from Csorna ■ 2011
59 x 37 inches (149.9 x 94 cm)
Cotton fabric, cotton thread, polyester batting;
hand quilted, appliquéd, pieced
PHOTO BY LÁSZLÓ JANTNER

MARGARET PHILLIPS CURLEY
Blue Light Special ■ 2002
72 x 72 inches (182.9 x 182.9 cm)
Cotton fabrics, cotton thread, polyester/cotton
batting; hand quilted, machine pieced
PHOTO BY PITTSBURGH CUSTOM DARKROOM

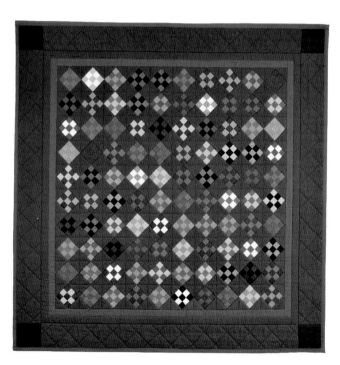

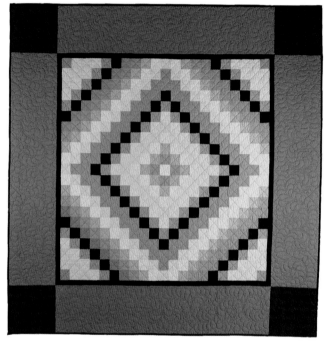

PETRA NIERMANN
Eulersches Quadrat ■ 2008
56 x 56 inches (142.2 x 142.2 cm)
Dyed bed linens; machine pieced and quilted
PHOTO BY GABRIELE NIEHAUS

BARBARA M. BURNHAM
Sunshine and Shadow Too ■ 2008
61½ x 63 inches (156.2 x 160 cm)
Cotton fabric, cotton thread, polyester
batting; hand quilted, pieced
PHOTO BY FABIANO REAN

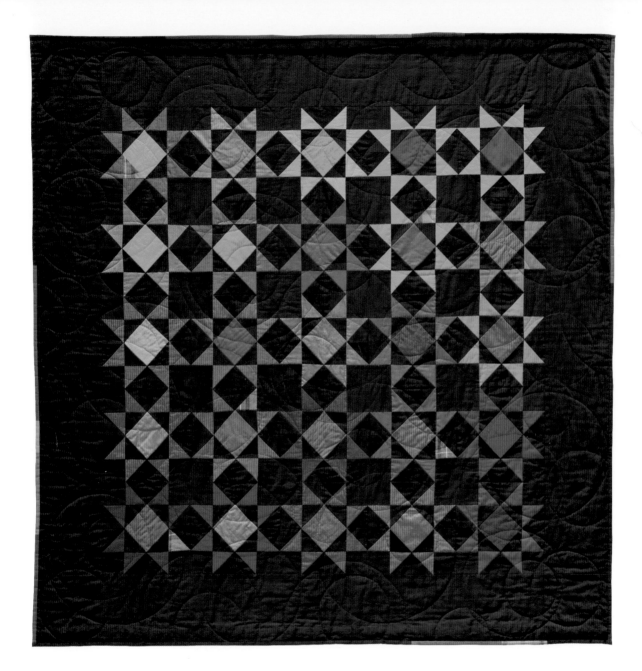

MAGGIE TURNER
Amish Stars ■ 1991

52 x 52 inches (132.1 x 132.1 cm)
Cotton fabric, cotton thread, cotton batting; machine quilted, pieced
PHOTO BY ARTIST

139

AILEYN RENLI ECOB

Appliqué Flower Block Quilt ■ 2002

104 x 91 inches (264.2 x 231.1 cm)
Cotton fabric, cotton thread, polyester batting;
hand quilted, hand appliquéd, machine pieced
BLOCKS AND PIECED BORDER DESIGNED BY BINKY BROWN TAKAHASHI
PHOTO BY LUKE MULKS

SHERRY REYNOLDS
America, Let It Shine ■ 2011

88 x 88 inches (223.5 x 223.5 cm)
Cotton fabric, hand-dyed fabrics, silk, cotton thread, silk thread, polyester
thread, cotton batting overlayed with wool batting, crystals; machine
quilted, hand and machine appliquéd, machine pieced, embellished
PHOTO BY JIM & JUDY LINCOLN

141

YUYIKO HIRANO
Baltimore Album II ■ 2000
82 x 82 inches (208.3 x 208.3 cm)
Cotton fabric, batting; hand appliquéd, pieced and quilted
PHOTO BY MIKE MCCORMICK

MARY KAY DAVIS
American All-Star ■ 2008
65 1/2 x 65 1/2 inches (166.4 x 166.4 cm)
Cotton fabric, cotton thread, cotton batting; machine
quilted, hand appliquéd, machine pieced
PHOTOS BY GREGORY CASE PHOTOGRAPHY

**HOLLY SWEET, MICHELLE BONDS,
TAMA BROOKS, KATHY HEFNER,
ROBERTA MILLER-HARAWAY, DOROTHY NEMY**
Star Banner ■ 2000
69 1/2 x 49 inches (176.5 x 124.5 cm)
Cotton fabric, cotton and metallic thread, cotton/
polyester batting; machine quilted, machine pieced
PHOTO BY MAGGIE WILSON

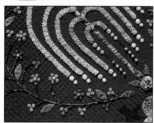

LINDA M. ROY
Wistful Willow ■ 2008
82 x 84 inches (208.3 x 213.4 cm)
Cotton, wool batting; hand appliquéd, hand quilted,
hand embroidered, ruching, machine pieced
PHOTOS BY ARTIST

KATHLEEN L. CARLSON
We're in a Pickle.... Practice the 4R's ■ 2012
35½ x 35½ inches (90.2 x 90.2 cm)
Cotton fabrics, cotton batiks, silk thread, cotton batting; machine quilted,
machine embroidered, hand and machine appliquéd, hand beaded
PHOTO BY ARTIST

CAROLE J. DUNKLAU
Virtues ■ 1999
86 x 86 inches (218.4 x 218.4 cm)
Cotton fabric, cotton thread, polyester batting; hand appliquéd,
hand quilted, machine pieced
QUILTED BY CAROL WURTH, DESIGN BY MURIEL DOUGLAS AND PATTY MILLER
PHOTO BY ARTIST

FAYE ANDERSON

Nouveau Abecedarian ■ 2002

51 x 51 inches (129.5 x 129.5 cm)
Cotton fabric, cotton thread, cotton batting;
hand quilted, appliquéd, pieced
PHOTO BY KEN SANVILLE

SUSAN H. GARMAN
Mama Said ■ 1999

87 x 73 inches (221 x 185.4 cm)
Cotton fabric, cotton thread, cotton batting;
hand quilted, appliquéd, pieced
PHOTOS BY JIM & JUDY LINCOLN

JANET STONE
B.S. I Love You ■ 2011

68 x 58 inches (172.7 x 147.3 cm)
Cotton fabrics, cotton, polyester and silk threads, 80/20
batting; machine pieced, appliquéd, quilted, embellished
PHOTOS BY JIM & JUDY LINCOLN

147

JANICE VAINE
Alphabet Sampler ■ 2011
89 x 89 inches (226.1 x 226.1 cm)
Cotton fabric, cotton and silk threads, silk ribbon, ombre wired ribbons, beads, wool
batting; hand appliquéd, silk ribbon embroidery, hand embroidered, ribbonwork

QUILTED BY MARILYN LANGE, STITCHED BY LUELLA M. DUSEK, JO ANN CRIDGE, SONNIE CRIDGE, GENA HOLLAND, JAN VAINE
COURTESY OF LANDAUER PUBLISHING
PHOTO BY SUE VOEGTLIN

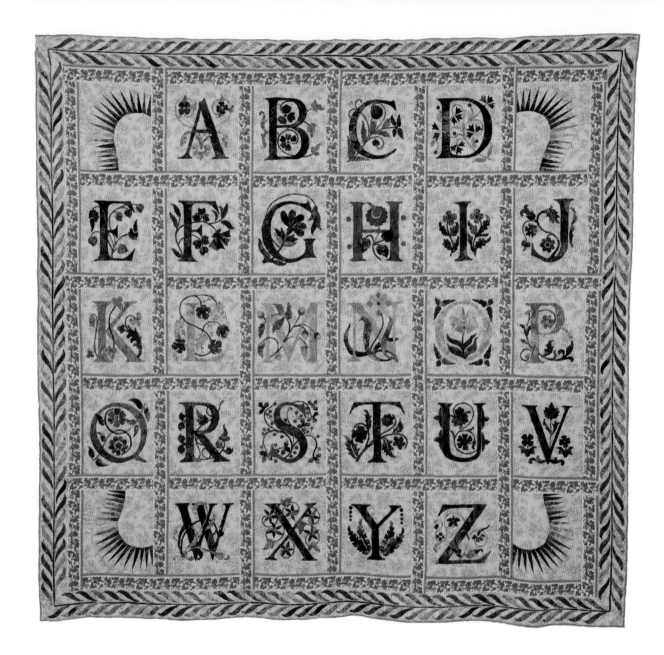

BARBARA KORENGOLD
An Alphabet ■ 2007–2008
80½ x 87 inches (204.5 x 221 cm)
Cotton fabric, cotton and silk thread, wool batting;
hand appliquéd, hand quilted, machine pieced
PHOTO BY RANDY SAGER

NAOKO HAYASHI
Joy of Pattern Lessons ■ 2005
79 x 70 inches (200.1 x 177.8 cm)
Cotton fabric; hand quilted, appliquéd, pieced
PHOTO BY TOSHIKATSU WATANABE

JANET STONE
Red Letter Daze ■ 2010

67 x 59 inches (170.2 x 149.9 cm)
Cotton fabric, cotton, silk, and polyester threads, wool batting; machine
quilted, appliquéd, pieced, free-motion embroidered, embellished
PHOTO BY JIM & JUDY LINCOLN

YOKO SAITO
Poinsettia ■ 2009
66 x 62 inches (167.6 x 157.5 cm)
Cotton fabric; hand quilted, appliquéd
PHOTO BY TOSHIKATSU WATANABE

ISAKO WADA
Landscape ■ 2004

83¼ x 83¼ inches (211.5 x 211.5 cm)
Cotton fabric, polyester thread, polyester batting;
hand quilted, pieced, appliquéd, embroidered
PHOTO BY ARTIST

153

DARLENE DONOHUE
Birds of a Feather ◼ 2009
82 x 70 inches (208.3 x 177.8 cm)
Cotton fabric, silk thread; hand appliquéd,
machine pieced, machine quilted
QUILTED BY DEBBIE YEZBAK
PHOTO BY CYNTHIA MCINTYRE

**JENNY CHIOVARO, BARBARA BAXTER, CAROL
ANN BARLEY, CAROLYN REINDL, MARY LOU COOPER,
ESTHER MIRTI, CAROL DECRUY, CAROL BELL**
Birds in the Garden ◼ 2009
90 x 90 inches (228.6 x 228.6 cm)
Cotton fabric, metallic thread; hand appliquéd, machine quilted
PATTERN BY NANCY MURTY, QUILTED BY NICOLE WEBB RIVERA
PHOTO BY MIKE MCCORMICK

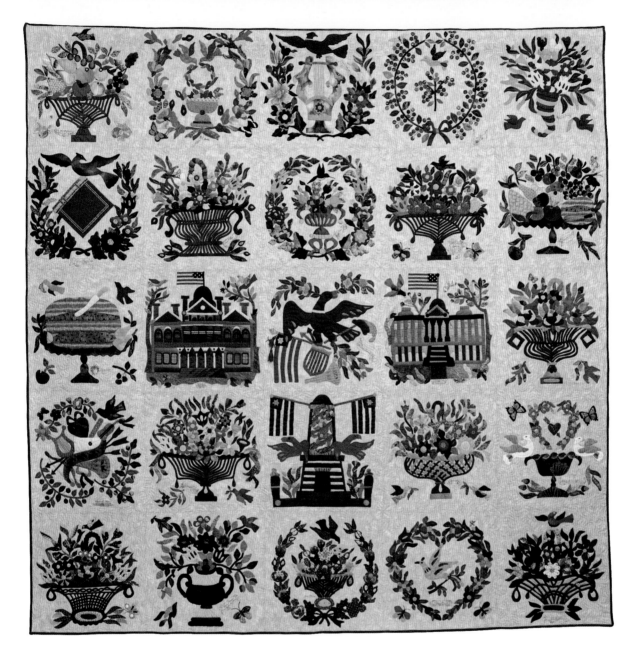

SANDRA L. MOLLON
Garden of Unity ■ 2009–2010
78¾ x 78¾ inches (200 x 200 cm)
Cotton fabric, silk and cotton thread, cotton batting;
machine quilted, hand appliquéd, machine pieced

QUILTED BY CREATIVE QUILTING OF GALT, CA
PHOTO BY ARTIST

KATHY K. WYLIE
Flourish on the Vine ■ 2011
73 x 62 inches (185.4 x 157.5 cm)
Cotton fabric, cotton, polyester, and nylon threads, wool and cotton/polyester blend
battings; hand appliquéd, hand and machine embroidered, domestic machine quilted
PHOTO BY ALEX ROBERTSON

KATHI CARTER
Andrew ■ 2012
92 x 92 inches (233.7 x 233.7 cm)
Cotton fabric, cotton thread, wool thread; machine appliquéd,
machine quilted and pieced
PHOTO BY ARTIST

157

BARBARA A. BLACK
A-Round with My Friends ■ 2011
67 x 67 inches (170.2 x 170.2 cm)
Cotton fabric, cotton thread, wool batting;
hand quilted, hand appliquéd, machine pieced
PHOTO BY JOSHUA BLACK WILKINS

JANET M. COCHRAN
Colorado Lily Garden ■ 2012

108 x 88 inches (274.3 x 223.5 cm)
Cotton fabric, cotton thread, cotton batting; hand appliquéd,
machine pieced, machine quilted

QUILTED BY STEPHANIE PATTERSON
PHOTO BY JOE COCA PHOTOGRAPHY

ISABELLE ETIENNE-BUGNOT
Mosaic Quilt ■ 2009
75 ⅝ x 75 ⅝ inches (192 x 192 cm)
Cotton fabric, cotton thread, cotton batting; hand pieced
PHOTO BY FRANCE PATCHWORK

LILIANE VERGER
Honey Comb ■ 2009
86 5/8 x 86 5/8 inches (220 x 220 cm)
Cotton fabric, cotton thread, cotton batting; English paper pieced
PHOTO BY FRANCE PATCHWORK

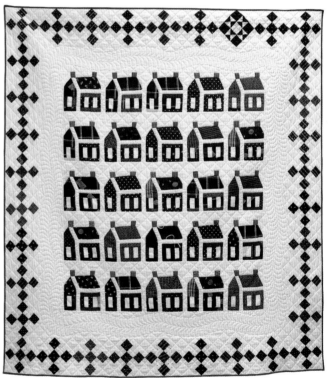

JANE BERGSTRALH
Dan's Freedom Quilt ■ 1996
81 x 81 inches (205.7 x 205.7 cm)
Cotton fabric, cotton thread, cotton batting;
hand appliquéd, machine pieced, hand quilted
PHOTO BY CRAIG MCDOUGAL

BARBARA M. BURNHAM
Welcome Home ■ 1989
67 x 60 inches (170.2 x 152.4 cm)
Cotton fabric, antique blocks, cotton thread, polyester
batting; hand quilted, hand pieced, machine assembled
PHOTO BY FABIANO REANI

KATHY K. WYLIE
The Lord Is My Shepherd ■ 2003

67 x 67 inches (170.2 x 170.2 cm)
Cotton fabric, cotton and nylon threads, cotton/polyester batting;
machine pieced, hand appliquéd, machine quilted

JUDY LAVAL MORTON
Indiana Starburst ■ Year Unknown
78 x 80 inches (198.1 x 203.2 cm)
Cotton fabric, cotton thread, batting; hand quilted, appliquéd, pieced
PIECED BY LYDIA STOLL
SET BY MIRIAM GRABER
PHOTO BY STRAUB PHOTOGRAPHY

MARIGOLD APPLIQUÉRS
For the Love of Appliqué ■ 2009–2012

90 x 90 inches (228.6 x 228.6 cm)
Cotton fabric, cotton and polyester thread, 80/20 cotton/polyester batting, beads; embellished, embroidered, 3D techniques, long-arm quilted, hand appliquéd, machine pieced

MARIGOLD APPLIQUÉRS: ZOË ALBERT, ELLA BECKETT, BETTE BERST, JEANNE CHAMBERS, LAWNA CLARK, GYL CONNATY, LOIS CONRADI, WILLA DALE, LYNDA DESROCHER, BRENDA ECKSTEIN, KAY FARINA, LILA FOLEY, VICTORIA GRAY, CAROL GREENHALGH, PAT HANSON, PEG HEATH, EARLA HORNE, GERALDINE HUBBARD, SANDRA LAUGHLAND, AUDREY MACKENZIE, MIEKE MCINTOSH, PAT OLMSTEAD, TINA PUTOTO, DOROTHY SCHULTE, LILLIAN SLYWKA, AUDREY VAILE, CELIA VISSCHER, LESLIE WELCH, SYLVIA WERNSEN, DOREEN WISHART, VAL WOJTULA
QUILTED BY DAVE ELLACOTT AND BEV BURKE
PHOTO BY MIKE MCCORMICK

JUDITH ROUSH KNORR
Midnight in the Garden of Hearts and Flowers ■ 2006
80 x 80 inches (203.2 x 203.2 cm)
Cotton fabric, cotton thread, batting; hand appliquéd, hand quilted
PHOTO BY ARTIST

MARIE-JOSEPHE VETEAU
Sur La Piste Du Mohican ■ 2011
61⅝ x 61⅝ inches (156.5 x 156.5 cm)
Cotton fabric, cotton thread, cotton batting;
hand quilted, pieced
PHOTO BY FRANCE PATCHWORK

MARGARET PHILLIPS CURLEY
Rising Star ■ 2007
88 x 88 inches (223.5 x 223.5 cm)
Cotton fabrics, cotton thread, polyester/cotton batting;
hand quilted, machine pieced, hand appliquéd
PHOTO BY PITTSBURGH CUSTOM DARKROOM

167

PATRICE PERKINS CRESWELL
Crewel Whirl ■ 1996
88 x 88 inches (223.5 x 223.5 cm)
Cotton fabric, cotton thread, batting; hand appliquéd, hand quilted
PHOTO BY JIM & JUDY LINCOLN

MARILYN BADGER
Green Sleeves ■ 2008

80 x 74 inches (203.2 x 188 cm)
Cotton and silk fabric, metallic and polyester thread;
machine pieced, machine appliquéd, machine quilted
DESIGNED AND PIECED BY CLAUDIA CLARK MYERS
COLLECTION OF THE NATIONAL QUILT MUSEUM OF THE UNITED STATES

PAT PETERS
Birds and Roses ■ 2009
86 x 86 inches (218.4 x 218.4 cm)
Cotton fabric, batiks, polyester batting, polyester thread,
cotton thread; hand appliquéd, hand quilted
PHOTO BY SHAUNA STEPHENSON

JOANNE JOHNSON
In the Garden with Morris and Hill ■ 2011
79 x 79 inches (200.7 x 200.7 cm)
Cotton fabric, cotton thread; hand and machine appliquéd,
hand embroidered, machine pieced and quilted
QUILTED BY KIM NORTON
PHOTO BY WILLIAM MORRIS & MICHELE HILL

NANCY C. ARSENEAULT
Happy, Happy, Happy ■ 2007
76 x 76 inches (193 x 193 cm)
Cotton fabrics, cotton and polyester threads, cotton
rickrack; machine appliquéd, machine quilted
PHOTO BY INTERNATIONAL QUILT ASSOCIATION

CINDY SEITZ-KRUG
Splendor in the Round ■ 2006
37 x 37 inches (94 x 94 cm)
Silk fabric, silk thread, wool batting; machine quilted
PHOTO BY TOM ALEXANDER

HAZEL CANNY
White Orchids ■ 2007
83 x 74 inches (210.8 x 188 cm)
Cotton sateen fabric, cotton thread, batting; hand quilted
PHOTOS BY JIM & JUDY LINCOLN

CATHLEEN MILLER
Inner Beauty ■ 2009

84 x 84 inches (213.4 x 213.4 cm)
Cotton fabric, cotton thread, silk thread, 80/20 batting;
hand quilted, hand appliquéd
PHOTO BY JIM & JUDY LINCOLN

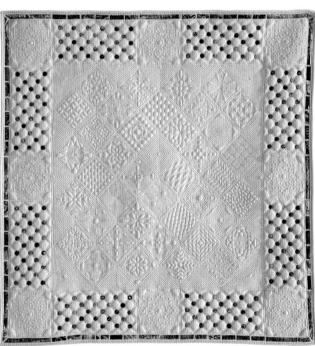

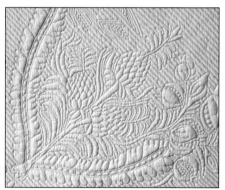

PENELOPE ROGER
Méli Mélo ▩ 2009
30 x 30 inches (76.2 x 76.2 cm)
Cotton fabric, cotton thread, cotton
batting; trapunto, hand quilted
PHOTO BY FRANCE PATCHWORK 08231

ANDREA PEREJDA
Homage to Provence ▩ 2008
28 x 46 inches (71.1 x 116.8 cm)
Cotton fabrics, cotton batting, cotton/
polyamide yarn; hand quilted,
hand stuffed, hand corded
PHOTOS BY ALAN EDELMAN 00531/00532

GEORGANN WRINKLE
Baltimore Woven Baskets ▨ 2013

59 x 59 inches (149.9 x 149.9 cm)
Cotton fabric, cotton thread, wool batting; needle-turn
appliquéd, machine pieced, machine quilted
QUILTED BY SUE GARMAN
PHOTO BY JULIE PAPPAN 07801/07802

175

LINDA STEELE
Crazy About Ballet ■ 2007
74 x 74 inches (188 x 188 cm)
Cotton fabric, cotton and silk thread, wool/polyester batting;
machine quilted, trapunto, hand embroidered, hand beaded
PHOTO BY ARTIST

KUMIKO FRYDL

Mission: Impeccable ■ 2010

18¼ x 18¼ inches (46.4 x 46.4 cm)
Cotton fabric, silk ribbon, cotton embroidery floss, rayon thread, silk thread,
cotton thread, cotton batting, cotton rickrack tape; paper foundation
pieced, reverse appliquéd, silk ribbon embroidered, machine quilted
PHOTO BY ARTIST

VICKI COODY MANGUM

Hot Pink Bird's Nest ■ 1995

88 x 88 inches (223.5 x 223.5 cm)
Cotton and silk fabrics, cotton, silk and embroidery threads, cotton/polyester batting;
machine pieced, hand appliquéd, hand quilted
PHOTO BY JIM & JUDY LINCOLN

CRISTINA SAKA
Spring Roses (Based on Kathy Nakajima Project) ■ 2006
80 x 80 inches (203.2 x 203.2 cm)
Hand appliquéd, hand pieced, hand quilted
PHOTO BY MEIRE MARQUES

179

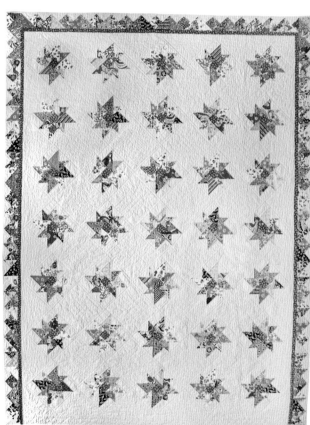

JOAN LEAHY BLANCHARD
Elisabeth's Wreath ■ 2011
82 x 63 inches (208.3 x 160 cm)
Cotton fabric, cotton thread, cotton batting;
machine quilted, hand pieced, appliquéd
QUILTED BY MAUREEN BLANCHARD
PHOTO BY JOANNA KEEFE

CAROL KOLF
Chicken Linen ■ 2005
104 x 80 inches (264.2 x 203.2 cm)
Cotton fabric (feed sacks), cotton thread,
cotton batting; hand quilted, pieced
PHOTO BY LAUREN MCCRIGHT

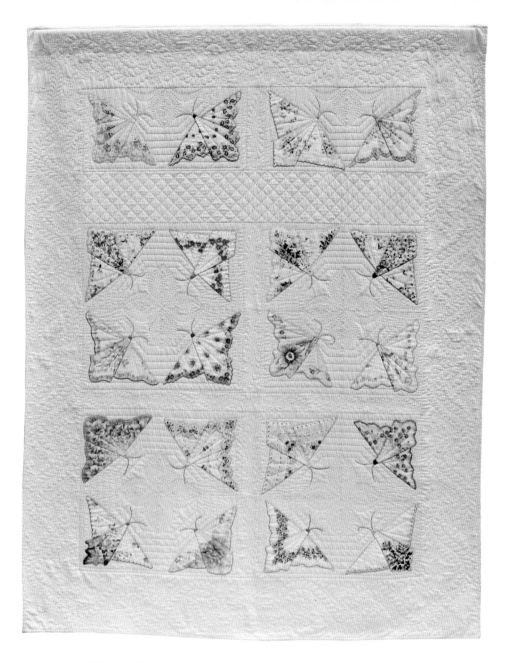

MARY C. FELDER
Butterfly Dance ■ 2009
96 x 72 inches (243.8 x 182.9 cm)
Vintage handkerchiefs, cotton fabric, cotton thread; hand appliquéd, quilted
QUILTED BY CAROL HILTON
PHOTO BY JUDY MOMENZADEH

181

ARDIE SKJOD
Butterflies ■ 2008
82 x 73 inches (208.3 x 185.4 cm)
Cotton fabrics, muslin, cotton thread, cotton batting;
pieced, embroidered, machine quilted
PHOTO BY TONI MARIE GARCIA

JENNY K. LYON
Stars 'n Stripes ■ 2012
46½ x 46½ inches (118.1 x 118.1 cm)
Cotton fabric, wool batting, metallic and silk thread;
free-motion quilted
PHOTO BY ARTIST

DIANE LOOMIS
KAREN PESSIA
May Tulips ■ 2009
24 x 24 inches (61 x 61 cm)
Cotton fabric, cotton and silk thread, wool and polyester batting;
machine quilted, trapunto, hand appliquéd, machine pieced
APPLIQUÉ DESIGN BY MARIE WEBSTER
PHOTO BY JOE OFRIA

BARBARA HOLTZMAN
Wishful Thinking ■ 2012
75 x 75 inches (190.5 x 190.5 cm)
Cotton fabric, silk, cotton, and polyester thread,
wool batting; machine quilted, pieced
PHOTOS BY ARTIST

SUZANNE MARSHALL
Miracles ■ 1988
91 x 78 inches (231.1 x 198.1 cm)
Cotton fabric, cotton-covered polyester thread, embroidery floss,
polyester batting; hand quilted, hand appliquéd, machine pieced
PHOTO BY CHARLES R. LYNCH

185

BONNIE RAYE KUCERA
The Posy Quilt ■ 2009
77 x 77 inches (195.6 x 195.6 cm)
Cotton fabric, cotton thread; hand quilted, hand appliquéd, machine pieced
PHOTO BY ARTIST

KRISTIN VIERRA
Passionately Purple ■ 2008
83 x 85 inches (210.8 x 215.9 cm)
Cotton fabric, cotton thread, cotton batting; machine
pieced, hand appliquéd, machine appliquéd
PHOTOS BY ARTIST

VENETTA MORGER
Wyoming Prairie Winters ■ 2009
89 x 83 inches (226.1 x 210.8 cm)
Cotton fabric, cotton thread, wool batting; pieced
PHOTO BY MIKE MCCORMICK

187

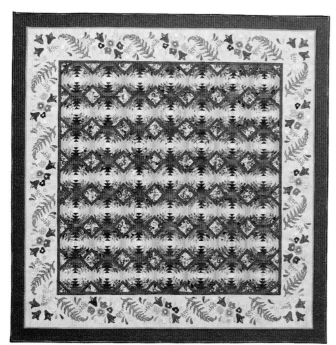

PATRICIA L. DELANEY
Inspiration Draws from Nature's Art ▨ 2008
80 x 80 inches (203.2 x 203.2 cm)
Cotton fabric, cotton thread, wool batting, acrylic yarn; machine pieced, paper pieced, machine appliquéd, hand couched, loop edged, trapunto, hand stitched, machine quilted
PHOTOS BY MATTHEW DELANEY

JAN SOULES
Bubblious ▨ 2010
67 x 67 inches (170.2 x 170.2 cm)
Cotton fabric, cotton thread, buttons, rickrack, 80/20 batting; long-arm quilted, pieced
QUILTED BY SHELLEY NEALON
PHOTO BY ARTIST

KIM MCLEAN
Princess Feathers ■ 2007

94 x 94 inches (238.8 x 238.8 cm)
Cotton; hand appliquéd and pieced, machine quilted
QUILTED BY KAY FERNIHOUGH
PHOTO BY TIM CONNOLLY

189

IRENE KNOWLES
Flowers of the Month Hawaiian Style ■ 2010
82 x 72 inches (208.3 x 182.9 cm)
Cotton fabric, cotton thread; hand quilted, hand appliquéd
COLLECTION OF RANDY AND JAN BRADY
PHOTO BY JOHN COLLINS

FACING PAGE **LEANNE HURLEY**
The Wonders of Nature ■ 2011–2012
94 x 74 inches (238.8 x 188 cm)
Needle-turn appliquéd, pieced, machine quilted
QUILTED BY ELVIRA ILLIG
PHOTO BY MIKE MCCORMICK

191

ANNA MARIA SCHIPPER-VERMEIREN
Stokrozen (Hollyhock) ■ 2011
64½ x 53½ inches (163.8 x 135.9 cm)
Cotton fabric, cotton thread, 80/20 cotton batting;
hand quilted, hand appliquéd, machine pieced
PHOTO BY HENK SCHIPPER

JENNY BACON
Birds in the Forest ■ 2010

53 x 53 inches (134.6 x 134.6 cm)
Cotton fabric, cotton thread, polyester batting;
hand appliquéd, machine pieced, hand quilted
PHOTO BY CHRIS MCDONALD

193

LAHALA PHELPS
Two Fond Hearts Unite ■ 2005
83 x 83 inches (210.8 x 210.8 cm)
Cotton fabric, cotton thread, polyester
batting; hand quilted, hand appliquéd
PHOTO BY MARK FREY

JANET HENSHAW
Flowers for My Valentine ■ 2011

92 x 91 inches (233.7 x 231.1 cm)
Cotton fabric, cotton and silk thread, cotton
batting; machine quilted, machine appliquéd
PHOTO BY JIM & JUDY LINCOLN

195

KIM MCLEAN
Roseville Album ■ 2009–2010

92 x 92 inches (233.7 x 233.7 cm)
Cotton; hand appliquéd and pieced, machine quilted
QUILTED BY KAY FERNIHOUGH
PHOTO BY TIM CONNOLLY

BARBARA KORENGOLD
Sew Is Life ■ 2008–2009

101 x 101 inches (256.5 x 256.5 cm)
Cotton and silk fabrics, cotton and silk threads, glass beads, wool batting;
hand appliquéd, hand embroidered, hand quilted, machine pieced
PHOTO BY PAUL ELBO

197

BARBARA KORENGOLD
Sam's Owl (A Mary Brown Album) ■ 2008–2011
101½ x 103 inches (257.8 x 261.6 cm)
Cotton fabrics, cotton and silk thread, wool batting; hand
appliquéd, hand embroidered, hand quilted, machine pieced
PHOTO BY PAUL ELBO

CYNTHIA COLLIER
Grace's Wedding Quilt ■ 2009
82 x 82 inches (208.3 x 208.3 cm)
Cotton fabrics, polyester batting; hand quilted, hand appliquéd
PATTERN BY JANE TOWNSWICK AND LISA SHILLER
PHOTO BY MIKE MCCORMICK

LYNN FOLLIS
Flower Bouquets ■ 2011
86 x 70 inches (218.4 x 177.8 cm)
QUILTED BY KAREN SHIVELY
PHOTO BY MIKE MCCORMICK

MICHELE A. BARNES
Pastorale ▧ 2011–2013
77 x 77 inches (195.6 x 195.6 cm)
Cotton fabric, cotton thread, batting; hand appliquéd,
hand embroidered, broderie perse
QUILTED BY RICHARD LARSON
PHOTO BY PHIL BARNES

GEORGANN WRINKLE
50th Wedding Anniversary ■ 2010

66 x 66 inches (167.6 x 167.6 cm)
Cotton fabric, cotton thread, wool batting, embroidery threads;
needle-turn appliquéd, machine pieced, machine quilted
QUILTED BY DENISE GREEN
PHOTO BY JULIE PAPPAN

MARGARET PHILLIPS CURLEY
All Around the Mulberry Bush ■ 2000
90 x 85 inches (228.6 x 215.9 cm)
Cotton fabric, polyester batting; machine
pieced, hand quilted, hand appliquéd.

JERRIANNE EVANS
Homeage to American Quilters ■ 2006
76 x 76 inches (193 x 193 cm)
Cotton fabric, cotton batting; hand appliquéd, machine pieced

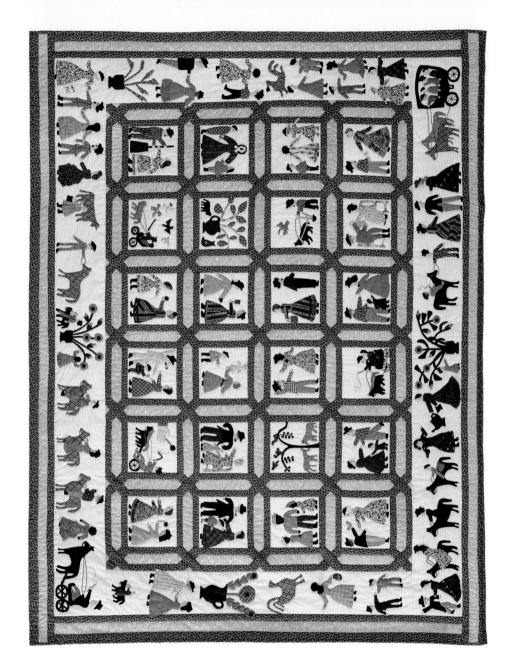

JOCELYNE PICOT
The Life of Phoebe Cook ■ 2009
66¹⁵/₁₆ x 59¹/₁₆ inches (170 x 150 cm)
Cotton fabric, cotton thread, cotton
batting; hand appliquéd
PHOTO BY FRANCE PATCHWORK

203

SANDRA L. MOLLON
Memories of Maryland ■ 1996–1998

82 x 82 inches (208.3 x 208.3 cm)
Cotton fabric, cotton threads, cotton batting;
hand quilted, hand appliquéd, machine pieced
PHOTO BY ARTIST

JANE BERGSTRALH
Texas Baltimore ■ 2011

88 x 88 inches (223.5 x 223.5 cm)
Cotton fabric, cotton thread, cotton/silk
batting; hand appliquéd, hand quilted
PHOTO BY CRAIG MCDOUGAL

SHIRLEY FOWLKES STEVENSON

Captain Tom, a Tall Texan ■ 1986

72 x 72 inches (182.9 x 182.9 cm)
Cotton fabric, thread, batting; hand
appliquéd, embroidered, quilted
PHOTO BY JIM & JUDY LINCOLN

207

CATHY BRADLEY
The Christmas Card Quilt ■ 2008
78 x 67 inches (198.1 x 170.2 cm)
Cotton fabric, cotton thread, cotton batting; hand quilted,
needle-turn appliquéd, embroidered
PHOTO BY JIM & JUDY LINCOLN

WEN REDMOND
First Star Farm ■ 1984
54 x 40 inches (137.2 x 101.6 cm)
Cotton fabrics, cotton thread, cotton
batting; hand quilted, pieced
PHOTO BY ARTIST

CAROLE L. CORDER
The Quilt Show ■ 2010
80 x 80 inches (203.2 x 203.2 cm)
Cotton fabric, cotton thread, cotton batting; hand quilted,
hand appliquéd, hand and machine pieced, hand embroidered
PHOTO BY ARTIST

MARGARETE HEINISCH
In the Heart of Europe ■ 1998

100 x 90 inches (254 x 228.6 cm)
Cotton, wool, silk, satin, blend of cotton/polyester, 80/20
batting; hand and machine pieced, hand appliquéd,
hand quilted, stuffed, embroidered, ink drawing
PHOTO BY MELLISA KARLIN MAHONEY

JANICE VAINE
Amuse-Bouche' ■ 2010

64 x 64 inches (162.6 x 162.6 cm)
Cotton fabric, silk, ultrasuede, wool, cotton and silk threads, silk ribbon,
ombre wired ribbon, beads, felt balls, wool batting; hand appliquéd, silk
ribbon embroidery, hand embroidered, ribbonwork, stumpwork

QUILTED BY MARILYN LANGE
STITCHED BY SUSAN B. ACHE, CAROLYN ALLEN, KAREN M. ALLISON, CHERYL P. ARMSTRONG, SUSAN BEADIN, VIRGINIA L.B. BECK,
KATHY BREIDENSTEIN, ANNETTE FLOCKHART BRINDLE, JO ANN CRIDGE, SONNIE CRIDGE, DORIS DOWLING, JOE DUSEK,
LUELLA M. DUSEK, SANDY AMADOR DUSEK, ELIN ELY, LOUISE FLOWERS, LYNN M. GRAHAM, GENA HOLLAND, N. GWEN LLOYD,
GLORIA PARSONS, BARBARA PONTE, LYNN ROGERS, DORIS EK SEELEY, SUSAN STIFF, RUTHE TOTH, JAN VAINE
COURTESY OF LANDAUER PUBLISHING
PHOTO BY SUE VOEGTLIN

HIROMI YOKOTA
Welcome to My House ■ 2002
79 x 71 inches (200.7 x 180.3 cm)
Cotton and wool fabric, polyester thread, polyester batting;
hand quilted, appliquéd, pieced, hand embroidered
PHOTO BY ARTIST

PAT KUHNS
Timeless Moments ■ 2010
26¹/₂ x 26¹/₂ inches (67.3 x 67.3 cm)
Cotton fabric, cotton thread, cotton batting;
needle-turn appliquéd, pieced
PHOTOS BY ARTIST

WEN REDMOND
Jonathan's Dream ■ 1985
40 x 40 inches (101.6 x 101.6 cm)
Cotton fabric, cotton thread, wool blanket batting;
hand quilted, hand appliquéd, hand pieced
PHOTO BY ARTIST

SUZANNE MOUTON RIGGIO
St. Mary's Visitation School: 1859–2009 ■ 2009
77 x 59 inches (195.6 x 149.9 cm)
Prismatic foil, cotton, silk, polyester, and nylon fabrics, cotton, silk and embroidery threads,
braids, beads, ultrasuede, glitter, lamé, ink, cords, oboe string; machine quilted
and embroidered, painted, hand embroidered, fused, machine and hand appliquéd,
machine pieced, couched, reverse appliquéd, beaded, computer printed fabrics
PHOTO BY ARTIST

ZENA THORPE
To England with Love ■ 1990

72 x 72 inches (182.9 x 182.9 cm)
Cotton fabric, cotton thread, polyester batting;
hand quilted, hand appliquéd
PHOTO BY DONALD LEVINE

KEIKO GOKE
My House ▪ 2008
77 x 77 inches (195.6 x 195.6 cm)
Cotton fabrics; machine pieced, quilted
PHOTO BY ARTIST

BETH CAMERON
My Kinda Town ■ 2011

90 x 80 inches (228.6 x 203.2 cm)
Cotton fabric, cotton thread, rayon thread, 80/20 batting;
machine quilted, pieced, appliquéd, embroidered
PHOTO BY RAY PILON

217

MARGARETE HEINISCH
And Crown Thy Good with Brotherhood ■ 2000

102 x 102 inches (259.1 x 259.1 cm)
Cotton fabric, cotton thread, silk thread, cotton batting, ink drawings;
hand appliquéd, hand embroidered, hand quilted
PHOTO BY JIM & JUDY LINCOLN

MARTHA MURILLO TSIHLAS
Texas DNA ■ 2010

55 x 55 inches (139.7 x 139.7 cm)
Cotton fabrics, batik fabrics, cotton thread, batting;
machine pieced, hand appliquéd, machine quilted
PHOTO BY JIM & JUDY LINCOLN

CINDY SEITZ-KRUG
Sew Long Sally ■ 2007
96 x 78 inches (243.8 x 198.1 cm)
Cotton fabric, cotton, rayon and monofilament thread,
wool batting; machine quilted, machine pieced
PHOTO BY TOM ALEXANDER

CAROL STAEHLE
Fleur de Lis ■ 2011

84 x 84 inches (213.4 x 213.4 cm)
Cotton fabrics; machine pieced, machine quilted
QUILTED BY SHERI MECOM
PHOTO BY ANNETTE PLOG

KUMIKO FRYDL
Monochromatic ■ 2011
14 x 14 inches (35.6 x 35.6 cm)
Polyester/cotton batiste, cotton fabric, polyester batting, cotton
thread, nylon thread, glitter thread, silk thread; machine quilted

500
traditional quilts

KRISTIN VIERRA
Magic of the Rose ■ 2011
94 x 82 inches (238.8 x 208.3 cm)
Cotton fabric, polyester thread, cotton batting;
machine appliquéd, machine quilted
PIECED BY JOAN WALDMAN, MARIE CLARK, GLORIA MILLER, AND SANDI KOSCH
PHOTO BY ARTIST

TED STORM
Spring of Desire ■ 2006
80 x 80 inches (203.2 x 203.2 cm)
Cotton and silk fabrics, cotton thread, perle cotton
thread, Shisha mirrors, beads, cotton batting; hand
pieced, hand appliquéd, embroidered, hand quilted
PHOTO BY JIM & JUDY LINCOLN

223

JANE HALL
Los Ventos ■ 1996
84 x 73 inches (213.4 x 185.4 cm)
Cotton fabric, cotton thread, polyester
batting; machine pieced, hand quilted
PHOTO BY RICHARD COX

HELEN REMICK

Untitled ■ 1996

90 x 90 inches (228.6 x 228.6 cm)
Cotton fabric, cotton thread, cotton batting;
hand quilted, appliquéd, and pieced
PHOTO BY MARK FREY

225

JUDY GARRISON SPAHN
Sunflowers ■ 2001
48 x 61 inches (121.9 x 154.9 cm)
Cotton fabric, cotton thread, cotton/polyester batting;
hand quilted, hand pieced
PHOTOS BY ARTIST

DIANA FAWN SHARKEY
Victorian Kaleidoscope ■ 2013

43 x 45½ inches (109.2 x 115.6 cm)
Cotton fabrics, cotton thread, cotton batting; pieced
QUILTED BY WILMA COGLIANTRY
PHOTO BY HOWARD GOODMAN

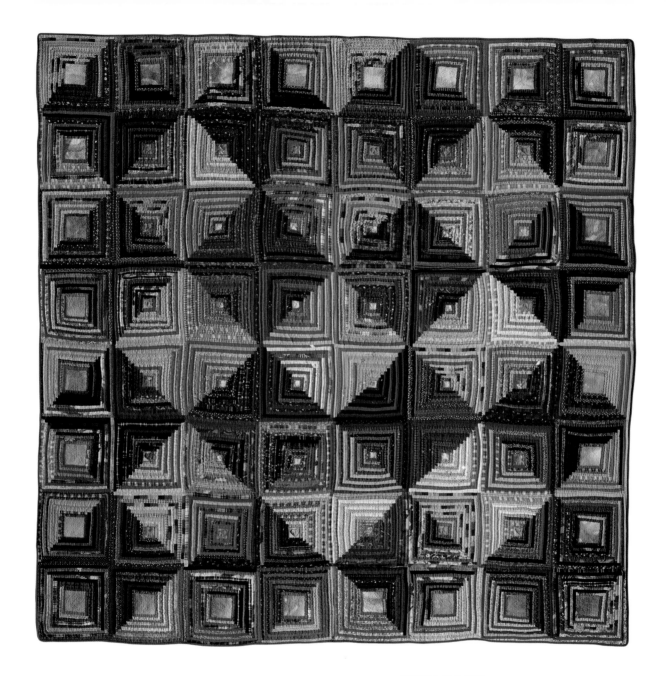

JUDY E. MARTIN
Something More Magical Than It Ever Was ▪ 1991
87 x 86 inches (221 x 218.4 cm)
Silk fabric, cotton fabric, cotton batting, recycled family clothing,
photo transfer, sequins, fabric paint; hand quilted, pieced
PHOTO BY MIKE MCCORMICK

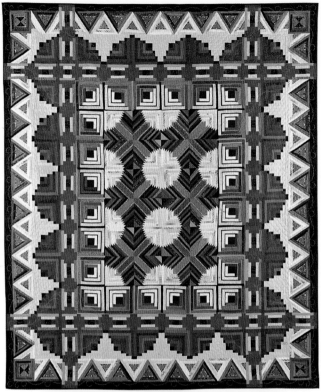

CLAUDIA CLARK MYERS
20th Century Silkie ■ 2000
102 x 89 inches (259.1 x 226.1 cm)
Dupioni silk, cotton fabric, rayon thread, 80/20
batting; machine quilted, machine pieced
PHOTOS BY JEFF FREY

TARA FAUGHNAN
Log Cabin Quilt ■ 2010
70 x 70 inches (177.8 x 177.8 cm)
Cotton fabrics, cotton thread, cotton/polyester
batting; machine pieced and quilted
PHOTO BY ARTIST

TIMNA TARR
Sunny Side Up ■ 2009
55 x 55 inches (139.7 x 139.7 cm)
Cotton fabric, cotton thread, wool batting; hand and
machine quilted, hand appliquéd, machine pieced
PHOTO BY STEPHEN PETEGORSKY

DIANNE FIRTH
Red Rectangle ■ 1997
39¹/₂ x 30 inches (100.3 x 76.2 cm)
Wool fabric, polyester embroidery thread, wool batting;
machine quilted, machine pieced
PHOTO BY ARTIST

JANET STEADMAN
Reflections at Sunset ■ 1988
87 x 67 inches (221 x 170.2 cm)
Cotton fabric, cotton thread, cotton
batting; hand quilted, hand pieced
PHOTO BY JIM & JUDY LINCOLN

231

SHARON SCHAMBER
Spirit of Mother Earth ■ 2008
99 x 99 inches (251.5 x 251.5 cm)
Hand-dyed cotton fabric, silk thread, wool batting;
machine application, machine pieced, corded, trapunto
PHOTO BY GENE SCHAMBER

MERELYN JAYNE PEARCE
Wheelflower Medallion ■ 2008
96½ x 96½ inches (245.1 x 245.1 cm)
Cotton fabric, cotton thread, monofilament thread, polyester batting;
hand appliquéd, hand embroidered, machine quilted
PHOTO BY UNKNOWN

233

DIANE LOOMIS
Square in Square I ■ 2010
14 x 14 inches (35.6 x 35.6 cm)
Cotton sateen and silk/cotton blend sateen fabric, silk
thread, wool batting; machine quilted, machine pieced
PHOTO BY JEFF LOMIKA

PETRA NIERMANN
Hexagramm ■ 2010
57 x 51 inches (144.8 x 129.5 cm)
Silk, lining, dyed bed linens;
machine pieced, quilted
PHOTOS BY GABRIELE NIEHAUS

JOAN DORSAY
Never Again...Again ■ 2009–2011

63 x 63 inches (160 x 160 cm)
Cotton fabric, cotton thread, cotton batting, cotton embroidery thread; hand appliquéd,
hand quilted, machine pieced, hand embroidered, dimensional appliquéd, stuffed, ruched
PHOTO BY ROLAND DORSAY

235

ANNA MARIA SCHIPPER-VERMEIREN
Dimensies ■ 2004
71¹/₂ x 59 inches (181.6 x 149.9 cm)
Cotton fabric, cotton thread, 80/20 cotton
batting; hand quilted, machine pieced
PHOTO BY HENK SCHIPPER

TIMNA TARR

Catena ■ 2011

62 x 67 inches (157.5 x 170.2 cm)
Cotton fabric, cotton thread, wool batting; hand and
machine quilted, hand appliquéd, machine pieced
PHOTO BY STEPHEN PETEGORSKY

237

NANCY L. BARDACH
Oh! Rock'a My Soul! (a "Rolling Wheel" variation) ■ 2008
56 x 82 inches (142.2 x 208.3 cm)
Cotton fabric, cotton and decorative polyester thread, 80/20 batting;
machine and hand quilted, pieced
PHOTO BY DON TUTTLE

PATRICIA L. DELANEY
Barcelona Crow's Nest ■ 2011

85½ x 96½ inches (217.2 x 245.1 cm)
Cotton fabric, cotton thread, wool batting, acrylic yarn;
machine pieced, machine quilted, hand couched, loop edged
PHOTO BY MATTHEW DELANEY

MARILYN BADGER
Euphoria ■ 2012
94 x 94 inches (238.8 x 238.8 cm)
Cotton and silk fabric, silk thread, cotton batting;
machine pieced, machine appliquéd, machine quilted
PHOTO BY ARTIST

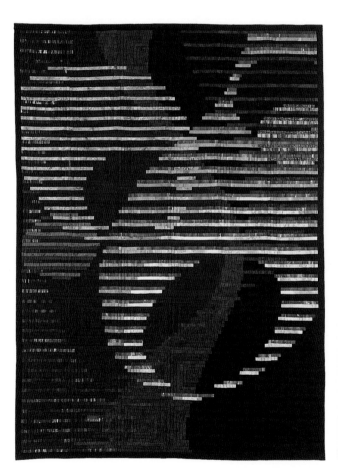
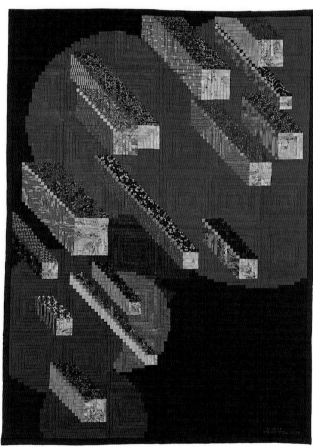

EMIKO TODA LOEB
Yuuyuu (Playful Abundance) front and back ■ 2008
82½ x 62 inches (209.6 x 157.5 cm)
Old and new cottons, cotton thread, cotton batting; pieced, quilted
PHOTOS BY KAREN BELL

LYNDA MARIE NOLL
Lake Reflections ■ 2005
91 x 81 inches (231.1 x 205.7 cm)
Cotton fabric, cotton thread; machine quilted, machine pieced
PHOTO BY ARTIST

MARGARET "PEGGY" FETTERHOFF
Sphere ■ 1999
92 x 92 inches (233.7 x 233.7 cm)
Pieced, hand quilted
PHOTO BY JIM & JUDY LINCOLN

243

SHIZUKO KUROHA
The Sky Away from Home ■ 2004
85 x 72 inches (215.9 x 182.9 cm)
Cotton fabric, cotton thread, polyester batting;
machine pieced, hand quilted
PHOTO BY AKINORI MIYASHITA

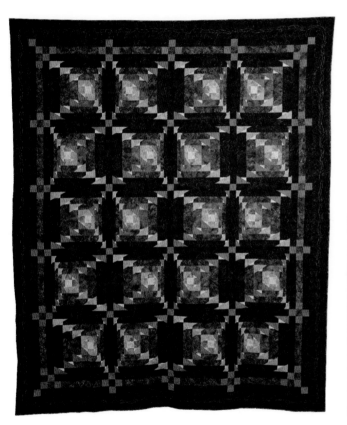

SUSAN CATANZARITO
Tulip Tango ■ 2011
109 x 91 inches (276.9 x 231.1 cm)
Cotton batik fabric; machine pieced, machine quilted
QUILTED BY ADRIA GOOD
PHOTO BY TIM HUFF

TADAKO NAGASAWA
Flower Bed ■ 2009
79 x 77 inches (200.7 x 195.6 cm)
Cotton fabric, cotton thread, wool batting; pieced, hand quilted
PHOTO BY MITSURU NAGASAWA

245

ANNA MARIA SCHIPPER-VERMEIREN
Purple ■ 2008
47¼ x 64⅛ inches (120 x 162.9 cm)
Cotton fabric, cotton thread, 80/20 cotton batting;
hand quilted, machine pieced, hand embroidered
PHOTO BY HENK SCHIPPER

500
traditional quilts

NANETTE L. STURGILL
Dreaming of Spring ■ 2012
65 x 54 inches (165.1 x 137.2 cm)
Cotton fabric, cotton thread, 80/20 batting,
paint sticks; hand quilted, appliquéd, stenciled
PHOTO BY DANNY LA PHOTOGRAPHY

SACHIKO YOSHIDA
Nadeshiko - Mother's Beloved Flowers ■ 2010
77⅛ x 77⅛ inches (196 x 196 cm)
Silk fabric, polyester and silk threads, polyester batting; hand quilted,
hand pieced, hand appliquéd, hand embroidered
PHOTO BY NOBUHIRO HONMA

YOSHIKO KOBAYASHI
Joy of Gardener ■ 2004
69 x 69 inches (175.3 x 175.3 cm)
Cotton, silk fabric, polyester thread, polyester batting;
machine quilted, appliquéd, embroidered, pieced
PHOTO BY SUN PHOTO STUDIO

249

SUSAN H. GARMAN
Ladies of the Sea ■ 2007

87 x 87 inches (221 x 221 cm)
Cotton fabric, cotton thread, cotton batting;
hand quilted, appliquéd, pieced
PHOTO BY JIM & JUDY LINCOLN

SARAH ANN SMITH
From the Schooner Coast ■ 2011
20½ x 20½ inches (52.1 x 52.1 cm)
Cotton fabric, polyester thread, batting; machine
quilted, machine pieced, fused appliqué
PHOTO BY ARTIST

SHELLY BURGE
Nebraska Navy ■ 2011
62 x 51½ inches (157.5 x 130.8 cm)
Cotton fabric, cotton thread, cotton batting;
machine quilted, machine pieced
QUILTED BY COLLEEN NOECKER
PHOTO BY ARTIST

SUSAN ATKINSON
Made with Love for Jane ▤ 2000–2011
77 x 77 inches (195.6 x 195.6 cm)
Cotton fabric, cotton thread, cotton batting;
machine pieced, hand appliquéd, hand quilted
PHOTO BY MARGARET HUTCHBY

MARY ARNOLD
North by Northeast ▤ 2005
19 x 19 inches (48.3 x 48.3 cm)
Cotton fabric, cotton thread, cotton batting;
paper pieced, micro machine quilted
PHOTO BY MARK FREY

DAWN FOX COOPER

Kootenay Compass ■ 2004

58 x 58 inches (147.3 x 147.3 cm)
Cotton fabric, cotton batting, cotton/polyester
thread; machine pieced, hand quilted
PHOTO BY MICHAEL MAYRHOFER

253

KUMIKO FRYDL
Nightcruise on the River Thames ▪ 2006
20½ x 20½ inches (52.1 x 52.1 cm)
Cotton fabric, cotton thread, cotton batting; hand quilted,
paper foundation pieced, machine pieced
PHOTO BY ARTIST

ANN L. PETERSEN
Sunlit Circles ■ 2011

74 x 74 inches (188 x 188 cm)
Cotton fabric, cotton, silk, nylon and polyester thread, cotton batting,
glass beads; machine quilted, machine pieced, hand beaded
PHOTO BY JIM & JUDY LINCOLN

255

MARY ARNOLD
Harmony ■ 2007
52 x 42 inches (132.1 x 106.7 cm)
Batik and cotton fabric, cotton thread, wool batting;
machine pieced, hand appliquéd, machine quilted
PHOTO BY MARK FREY

CLAUDIA CLARK MYERS

Sparkle Plenty ■ 2003

95 x 95 inches (241.3 x 241.3 cm)
Cotton fabric, rayon thread, 80/20 batting; long-arm machine quilted, machine pieced
QUILTED BY MARILYN BADGER
PHOTO BY JEFF FREY

MADELEINE VAIL
Autumn Memories ■ 2013
113 x 105 inches (287 x 266.7 cm)
Cotton fabric, cotton, polyester, and metallic threads,
cotton batting; machine quilted, appliquéd, pieced
PHOTO BY TIM MURPHY

FACING PAGE **BRIGITTE MORGENROTH**
Weitverzweigt (Widely Ramified) ■ 2010
85¾ x 57½ inches (217.8 x 146.1 cm)
Silk fabric, polyester thread, polyester
batting; hand quilted, paper pieced
PHOTO BY ALBRECHT MORGENROTH

259

PATRICIA T. MAYER
Opposites Attract ■ 2007
54 x 54 inches (137.2 x 137.2 cm)
Cotton fabric, silk and cotton threads; hand appliquéd, machine quilted
QUILTED BY KAREN WATTS
COURTESY OF INTERNATIONAL QUILT ASSOCIATION
PHOTO BY JIM & JUDY LINCOLN

CHRISTINE M. RUSSELL
Fall in Twain Harte ■ 2008
65 x 63 inches (165.1 x 160 cm)
Cotton batik fabrics, machine appliquéd, machine pieced, quilted
QUILTED BY DEE SMALL
PHOTO BY ARTIST

YOKO SAITO
Fagel Pipa ■ 2011
75 x 68 inches (190.5 x 172.7 cm)
Cotton fabric; hand quilted, appliquéd
PHOTO BY TOSHIKATSU WATANABE

YOSHIKO KOBAYASHI
Rambler Rose ■ 2006
72 x 70 inches (182.9 x 177.8 cm)
Cotton fabric, polyester thread, polyester batting; machine quilted, appliquéd, pieced
PHOTO BY SUN PHOTO STUDIO

263

MARY HUNTINGTON
Mighty Oak ▪ 2004
98 x 98 inches (248.9 x 248.9 cm)
Hand-dyed silk ribbon, fabric, batting; embroidered,
tatted, appliquéd, Brazilian embroidered
PHOTO BY MIKE MCCORMICK

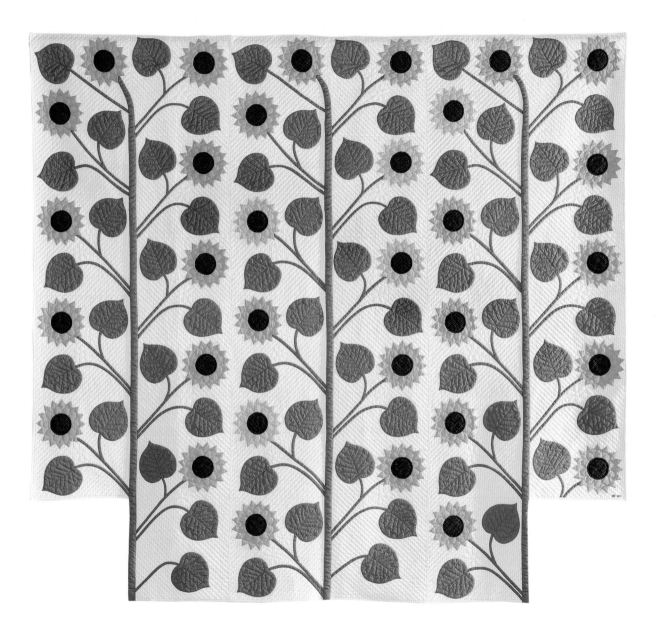

EWA GUERIN

Sun Flower ■ 2009

84¼ x 76⅜ inches (214 x 194 cm)
Cotton fabric, cotton thread, cotton batting; hand pieced
PHOTO BY FRANCE PATCHWORK

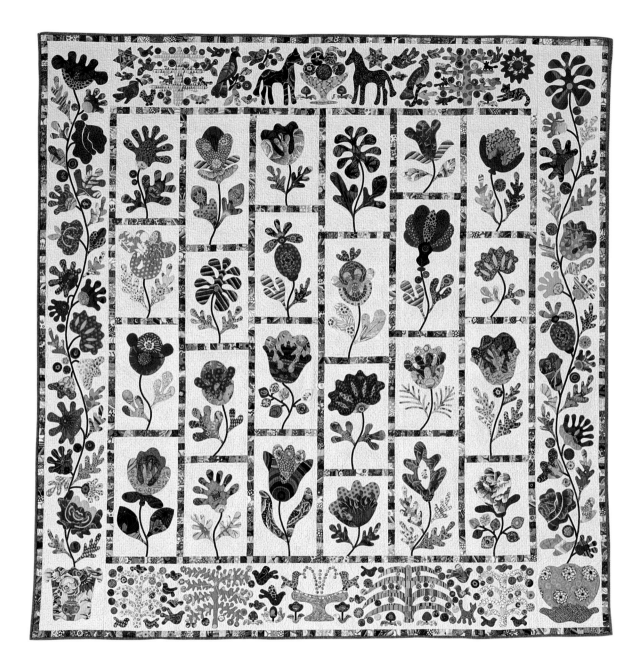

KIM MCLEAN
The Garden ▨ 2009–2010
91 x 89 inches (231.1 x 226.1 cm)
Cotton; hand appliquéd and pieced, machine quilted
QUILTED BY KAY FERNIHOUGH
PHOTO BY TIM CONNOLLY

FACING PAGE **HAZEL J. KITTS**
United Flowers of America ▨ 2002–2012
90 x 76 inches (228.6 x 193 cm)
Cotton fabric, cotton thread, cotton
batting; hand quilted
PHOTO BY JEREMIAH GUELZO

267

BARBARA ANN BAUER BARRETT
The Forest and the Trees ■ 2004
82 x 79 inches (208.3 x 200.7 cm)
Cotton fabric, cotton thread, cotton batting; hand
appliquéd, machine pieced, hand and machine quilted
PHOTO BY JIM & JUDY LINCOLN

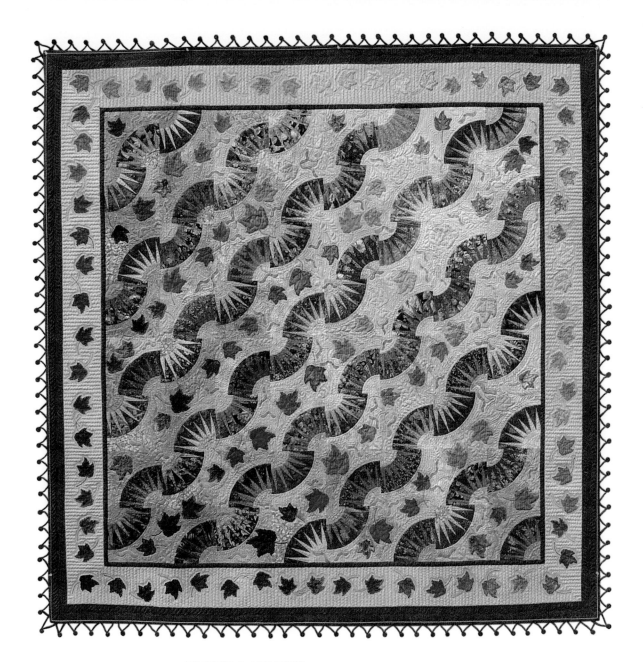

PATRICIA L. DELANEY
Sugar Maples and Nose Stickers ■ 2009

86 x 86 inches (218.4 x 218.4 cm)
Cotton fabric, cotton thread, rayon thread, wool batting,
acrylic yarn; machine pieced, machine embroidered, machine
appliquéd, machine quilted, hand stitched, hand couched
PHOTO BY MATTHEW DELANEY

HAZEL CANNY
Romanesque Flourishes ■ 2008
96 x 77 inches (243.8 x 195.6 cm)
Cotton sateen fabric, cotton thread,
batting; hand quilted
PHOTO BY JIM & JUDY LINCOLN

MIEKO KOTAKI
Tenderly Embraced ■ 2009
79 1/2 x 79 1/2 inches (201.9 x 201.9 cm)
Cotton fabric; hand quilted, appliquéd, pieced, embroidered
PHOTO BY EMIKO ŌNUMA

YOKO SAITO
Nantucket Basket ■ 2009
73 x 68 inches (185.4 x 172.7 cm)
Cotton fabric; hand quilted, appliquéd
PHOTO BY TOSHIKATSU WATANABE

TERRI DOYLE
A Touch of Autumn ■ 2010
18 x 18 inches (45.7 x 45.7 cm)
Cotton fabric, wool batting, silk thread; whole cloth machine quilted
PHOTO BY ARTIST

LAURIE WEINER
Tournesol ■ 2009

31 x 29 inches (78.7 x 73.7 cm)
Hand-dyed cotton sateen fabric, cotton thread, polyester batting,
cotton batting; trimmed trapunto, freehand machine quilted
PHOTO BY MICHELE STADLER

TERRI DOYLE
Secret Garden ■ 2011
71 x 71 inches (180.3 x 180.3 cm)
Cotton fabric, batting; machine quilted
PHOTO BY JIM & JUDY LINCOLN

ANDREA PEREJDA
Silver Splendor ■ 2000
80 x 80 inches (203.2 x 203.2 cm)
Cotton sateen, cotton thread, poly-down batting; hand quilted
PHOTO BY ALAN EDELMAN

KUMIKO FRYDL
Mission: Impossible 2 ■ 2009
11³⁄₄ x 11³⁄₄ inches (29.8 x 29.8 cm)
Cotton fabric, silk thread, thread, cotton rickrack tape, cotton batting;
paper foundation pieced, reverse appliquéd, machine quilted
PHOTO BY ARTIST

ANN T. PIGNERI
Caroline ■ 2011
23 inches (58.4 cm) in diameter
Silk and cotton blend fabric, silk thread, wool batting;
free-motion machine quilted, whole cloth
PHOTO BY RICK WARD

DIANE LOOMIS
Five Bar Blues ■ 2010
65 x 50 inches (165.1 x 127 cm)
Cotton and silk/cotton blend sateen fabric, cotton and silk thread,
wool batting; machine quilted, trapunto, machine pieced
PHOTO BY INTERNATIONAL QUILT ASSOCIATION

LAURIE WEINER
Arabesque ■ 2009

38 x 30½ inches (96.5 x 77.5 cm)
Hand-dyed cotton sateen fabric, polyester batting, wool batting, cotton thread;
wholecloth, drawn, cut-away trapunto, free-hand machine stitched
HAND-DYED COTTON SATEEN FABRIC BY JEANETTE VIVIANO
PHOTO BY MICHAEL STADLER

JANE HALL
Piko Haleakala ■ 1975
84 x 83 inches (213.4 x 210.8 cm)
Cotton/polyester fabric, polyester batting;
hand appliquéd, hand quilted
PHOTO BY RICHARD COX

YACHIYO KATSUNO
Thank You Quilt ■ 2011
86 5/8 x 86 5/8 inches (220 x 220 cm)
Cotton fabric, polyester thread, polyester
batting; hand quilted, hand appliquéd
PHOTO BY KOO SAITO

279

SARAH ANN SMITH
Nourish the Body, Nourish the Soul ■ 2008
64 x 64 inches (162.6 x 162.6 cm)
Cotton fabric, polyester thread, batting;
machine quilted, machine appliquéd
PHOTO BY ARTIST

CINDY SEITZ-KRUG
Passion at Midnight ■ 2003

84 x 84 inches (213.4 x 213.4 cm)
Cotton fabric, rayon thread, 80/20 polyester/cotton batting;
machine quilted, hand appliquéd
PHOTO BY TOM ALEXANDER

281

MARLINE TURNER
Salisbury 'n Cream ■ 2008
79 x 79 inches (200.7 x 200.7 cm)
Cotton fabric, silk thread, batting; hand quilted, hand appliquéd
PHOTO BY ARTIST

KIT ROBINSON
Endless Hawaiian Quilt ■ 2001

88 x 88 inches (223.5 x 223.5 cm)
Batiks, cotton fabrics, rayon and polyester/cotton threads;
hand appliquéd, machine quilted
PHOTO BY GREGORY CASE PHOTOGRAPHY

MÁRIA MOLNÁR JÁNOSNÉ
Tulips from Buzsak ■ 2010
32 x 27 inches (81.3 x 68.6 cm)
Cotton fabric, cotton thread, polyester batting;
hand quilted, appliquéd, pieced
PHOTO BY LÁSZLÓ JANTNER

CHRISTINE N. BROWN
Hawaiian Blue ■ 2012
24 x 24 inches (61 x 61 cm)
Hand-dyed cotton fabric, cotton thread;
hand appliquéd, machine quilted
QUILTED BY SHERRY REYNOLDS
PHOTO BY CHARLES R. LYNCH

SARAH ANN SMITH
Haleakala Sunrise ■ 2003
42 x 42 inches (106.7 x 106.7 cm)
Hand-dyed cotton, polyester thread, batting;
machine quilted, machine appliquéd
PHOTO BY ARTIST

DEBBY TRACY WALTERS
Bright Nights ■ 2012

82 x 82 inches (208.3 x 208.3 cm)
Cotton fabric, cotton thread, cotton batting;
machine quilted, trapunto, pieced

PATTERN FROM RAINBOW GALAZY BY PEGGY MARTIN AND STAR
PATTERNS BY CAROL DOAK, QUILTED BY ROSANN GILBERT
PHOTO BY ARTIST

SUSIE L. ANDERSEN
MARGIE L. LAMBETH
Spring Garden ■ 2010

88 x 74 inches (223.5 x 188 cm)
Cotton fabric, cotton thread, cotton batting; machine quilted, pieced

QUILTED BY MARGARET A. PHILLIPS
PHOTO BY JIM & JUDY LINCOLN

MADELEINE VAIL
Radiating Star ■ 2002
100 x 100 inches (254 x 254 cm)
Cotton fabric, cotton thread, cotton batting;
machine quilted, pieced
PHOTO BY TIM MURPHY

JUDY LAVAL MORTON
Miss Refrigeradorables' Album Quilt ■ 2000–2010
96 x 112 inches (243.8 x 284.5 cm)
Cotton fabric, cotton thread, wool batting; hand quilted, appliquéd, pieced
PHOTO BY STRAUB PHOTOGRAPHY

MARY ALYCE BORDELON
My Pride and Joy ■ 2012
91 x 91 inches (231.1 x 231.1 cm)
Cotton fabric, nylon thread, polyester batting;
machine quilted, hand appliquéd, machine pieced
QUILTED BY RUBY MIRE
PHOTO BY DAN DIEFENDERFER

JUDY LAVAL MORTON
Somewhere in Time ■ 1998-2000
110 x 110 inches (279.4 x 279.4 cm)
Cotton fabric, cotton thread, wool batting; hand quilted, appliquéd, pieced
PHOTO BY MICHAEL WHEATLEY

LAHALA PHELPS
Journey Hand in Hand ■ 2007
94 x 94 inches (238.8 x 238.8 cm)
Cotton fabric, cotton thread, polyester batting;
hand quilted, hand appliquéd
PHOTO BY MARK FREY

BARBARA ANN MCCRAW
Paradiso ■ 2008
78 x 78 inches (198.1 x 198.1 cm)
Cotton fabric, thread, 80/20 batting; hand appliquéd,
machine pieced, machine quilted
QUILTED BY JOHANNA IAIA
PHOTO BY GUY T

FACING PAGE **KATHI CARTER**
Emily ■ 2010
86 x 86 inches (218.4 x 218.4 cm)
Cotton fabric, cotton thread, 80/20 batting;
machine appliquéd, machine quilted,
machine pieced, hand ruched
PHOTO BY JIM & JUDY LICOLN

293

PAT PETERS
Hearts and Tulips ■ 2011
65 x 65 inches (165.1 x 165.1 cm)
Cotton fabric, batiks, polyester batting, polyester thread,
cotton thread; hand appliquéd, hand quilted
PHOTO BY SHAUNA STEPHENSON

CLAUDIA CLARK MYERS
Awesome Blossom ■ 2007

94 x 94 inches (238.8 x 238.8 cm)
Cotton fabric, rayon thread, 80/20 and silk batting; long-arm
machine quilted, machine pieced, machine appliquéd
QUILTED BY MARILYN BADGER
PHOTOS BY ARTIST

VICKI COODY MANGUM
Airbrushed Appliqué ■ 1993

42 x 42 inches (106.7 x 106.7 cm)
Cotton and silk fabrics, hand-dyed fabrics, cotton and
embroidery threads, cotton/polyester batting; hand appliquéd,
hand quilted, hand embroidered, machine quilted
PHOTO BY MIKE MCCORMICK

SHELLY PAGLIAI
Passion's Flowers ■ 2004
86 x 86 inches (218.4 x 218.4 cm)
Cotton fabric, polyester thread, polyester batting;
hand appliquéd, machine pieced, hand quilted
PHOTO BY ANGELA MASSIE

MERELYN JAYNE PEARCE
Wildflowers of Margaret Preston ■ 2005
56¼ x 53 inches (142.9 x 134.6 cm)
Cotton fabrics, cotton thread, monofilament thread, polyester
batting; hand appliquéd, hand embroidered, machine quilted
PHOTO BY UNKNOWN

CHERYL KERESTES
Rose Album ■ 2007
98 x 98 inches (248.9 x 248.9 cm)
Cotton fabric, cotton thread, polyester batting;
hand appliquéd, hand quilted, machine pieced
PHOTO BY MOWRY PHOTO STUDIO

MICHELE A. BARNES
Lapis Vessels ■ Year Unknown
75 x 75 inches (190.5 x 190.5 cm)
Cotton fabrics, cotton thread, wool batting; hand
quilted, hand appliquéd, machine assembled
PHOTO BY JIM & JUDY LINCOLN

STEVII GRAVES
MARTHA NORDSTRAND
The Yellow Rose of Texas and More ■ 2011
91 x 81 inches (231.1 x 205.7 cm)
Cotton fabric, cotton and silk thread; hand appliquéd, machine quilted
QUILTED BY MEREDYTH GRETZINGER ROTLISBERGER
PHOTOS BY INTERNATIONAL QUILT ASSOCIATION

ZENA THORPE
Frogmore ■ 1994
92 x 92 inches (233.7 x 233.7 cm)
Cotton fabric, cotton thread, cotton batting; hand quilted, hand appliquéd
PHOTO BY DONALD LEVINE

GEORGINA BUSCHAUER
Challenge 1 ■ 2008
89½ x 74¼ inches (227.3 x 188.6 cm)
Cotton fabric, cotton thread, cotton batting; hand quilted,
hand appliquéd, machine pieced
PHOTO BY MIKE MCCORMICK

GAIL VALENTINE
Blooming Nosegay ■ 2000
99 x 61½ inches (251.5 x 156.2 cm)
Machine pieced, machine appliquéd, machine quilted
PHOTOS BY ARTIST

ANNETTE PLOG
Green Baskets ■ 2004
96 x 84 inches (243.8 x 213.4 cm)
Cotton fabric, cotton batting; hand quilted
PHOTO BY ARTIST

ANNA MARIA SCHIPPER-VERMEIREN
Wisteria (Blauwe regen) ■ 2011
65¼ x 56⅝ inches (165.7 x 143.8 cm)
Cotton fabric, cotton thread, 80/20 cotton batting; hand quilted,
appliquéd, machine pieced, hand embroidered
PHOTO BY HENK SCHIPPER

LIZ JONES
Heart and Garlands ■ 2007

76 x 76 inches (193 x 193 cm)
Cotton fabric, rayon appliqué thread, wool batting,
silk thread; free-motion machine quilted
PHOTO BY NEIL PORTER

303

DAVID WOTRUBA
My Hawaiian Garden ■ 2013
81 x 85 inches (205.7 x 215.9 cm)
Cotton fabric, cotton thread, polyester
batting; hand quilted, appliquéd
DESIGN BY EMMA CEBERANO
PHOTO BY GLEN DAVIS AND ASSOCIATES

LYNN W. CARRICO
Blossoms in the B. A. ■ 2002
72 x 60 inches (182.9 x 152.4 cm)
Machine pieced, hand appliquéd, machine quilted
PHOTOS BY ARTIST

MERELYN JAYNE PEARCE
Tribute to Margaret Preston ■ 2002

94 x 94 inches (238.8 x 238.8 cm)
Cotton fabric, cotton thread, monofilament thread, polyester batting;
hand appliquéd, hand embroidered, trapunto, machine quilted
PHOTO BY UNKNOWN

JANET M. COCHRAN
Christy's Cabin ■ 2011
101 x 87 inches (256.5 x 221 cm)
Cotton fabric, cotton thread, cotton
batting; machine pieced and quilted
QUILTED BY STEPHANIE PATTERSON
PHOTO BY JOE COCA

ANNETTE PLOG
Union Square ■ 2003
80 x 65 inches (203.2 x 165.1 cm)
Cotton fabric, cotton batting; hand quilted
PHOTOS BY ARTIST

SUSAN WEBB LEE

Versicolor ■ 2011

30½ x 30½ inches (77.5 x 77.5 cm)
Hand-dyed, painted and commercially printed cotton
fabrics, cotton embroidery floss, cotton/polyester
thread, cotton batting; hand quilted, appliquéd, pieced
PHOTO BY STEVE MANN

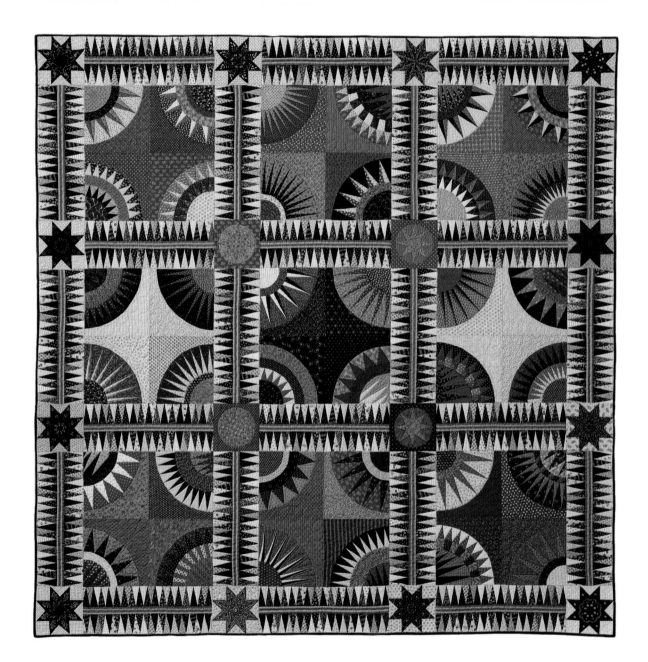

PATRICIA T. MAYER
New York Jazz ▦ 2010
74 x 74 inches (188 x 188 cm)
Cotton fabric, cotton thread, cotton batting;
machine pieced, hand appliquéd, machine quilted
QUILTED BY KAREN WATTS
PHOTO BY INTERNATIONAL QUILT ASSOCIATION

ANN HORTON
Tradewinds to the Orient ■ 2002

86 x 75 inches (218.4 x 190.5 cm)
Cotton fabrics, cotton lamé, blended drapery fabric,
cotton, rayon, and metallic threads, cotton batting; hand
and machine quilted, machine pieced, hand beaded
PHOTO BY EVAN JOHNSON

JANET STONE
Alpha'baa't Sampler ■ 2009
87½ x 64 inches (222.3 x 162.6 cm)
Cotton fabric, cotton thread, 80/20 fusible batting;
machine pieced, appliquéd, and quilted, embellished
PHOTO BY JIM & JUDY LINCOLN

BARBARA JAHN
African Sampler ■ 2010
95½ x 80 inches (242.6 x 203.2 cm)
African cotton remnants, cotton thread, polyester batting;
machine pieced, hand appliqéd, hand quilted
PHOTO BY CARLOS TOBON

REBECCA ROHRKASTE
Binding Memories ■ 1991

84 x 84 inches (213.4 x 213.4 cm)
Cotton fabric, cotton thread, cotton
batting; hand quilted, machine pieced
PHOTO BY SHARON RISEDORPH

311

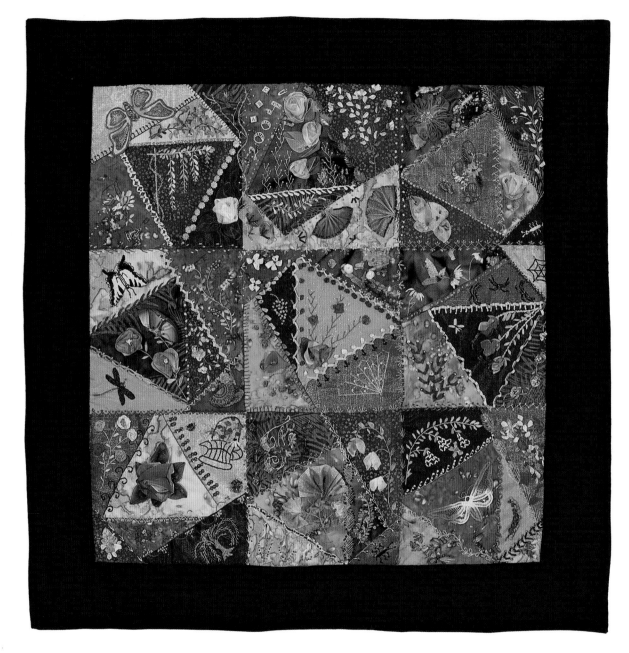

JUNE F. SILBERMAN
My Very Own Crazy Quilt ■ 2004
32 x 32 inches (81.3 x 81.3 cm)
Metallic fabric, silk ribbon, embroidery floss, beads, buttons, charms,
needle lace, cotton fabric, cotton thread, wired ribbon
PHOTO BY ANDREW GILLIS

SHELLY BURGE
Star Light - Star Bright ■ 2006
38½ x 47 inches (97.8 x 119.4 cm)
Cotton fabric, cotton thread, cotton
batting; machine quilted, machine pieced
PHOTO BY ARTIST

313

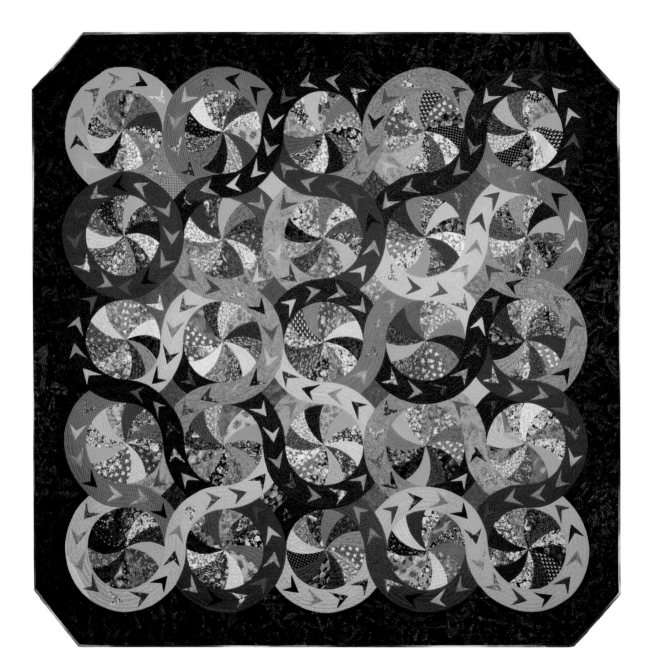

CINZIA WHITE
Trails ■ *2*004
114 x 114 inches (289.6 x 289.6 cm)
Cotton fabric, cotton thread, wool/polyester
batting; hand quilted, hand pieced
PHOTO BY ANTHONY BURNS

SACHIKO YOSHIDA
Spellbound Silk Balls ■ 2007
78 3/4 x 78 3/4 inches (200 x 200 cm)
Silk fabric, polyester and silk threads, polyester batting; hand quilted,
hand pieced, hand appliquéd, hand embroidered
PHOTO BY NOBUHIRO HONMA

315

DAWN FOX COOPER
Flower Garden ■ 2011
13 x 13 inches (33 x 33 cm)
Mixed synthetic fabrics, cotton and polyester thread,
wool batting, polyester ribbon, glass beads;
hand quilted with French knots
PHOTO BY ARTIST

DOMINIQUE HUSSON
Losange de Fleurs ■ 2009
82 ¹¹/₁₆ x 68 ¹⁵/₁₆ inches (210 x 175 cm)
Cotton fabric, cotton thread,
cotton batting; hand pieced
PHOTOS BY FRANCE PATCHWORK

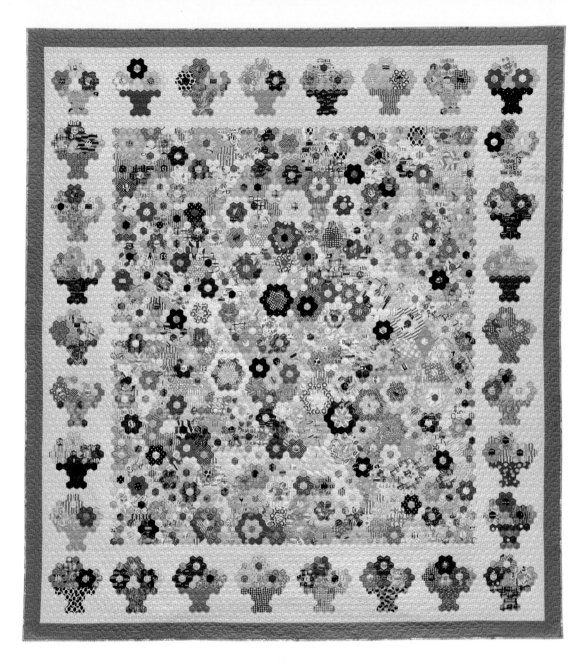

SUZUKO KOSEKI
Compote of Flowers ■ 2011
91 x 83 inches (231.1 x 210.8 cm)
Cotton fabric, silk fabric, cotton thread,
polyester batting; hand quilted, pieced
PHOTO BY ARTIST

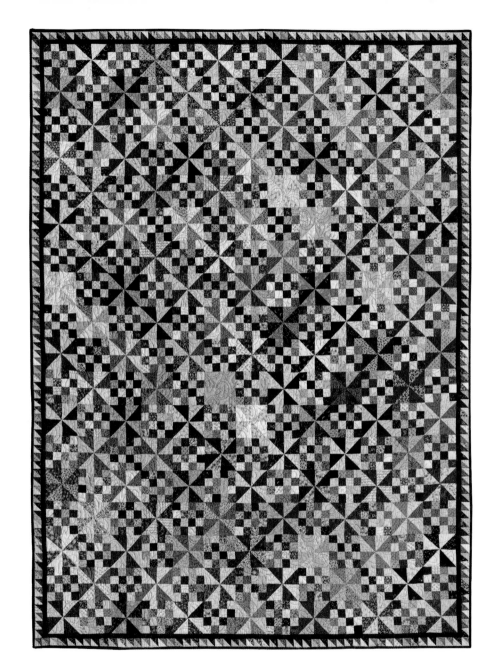

NONA C. FLORES
Prairie Pinwheels ■ 2011
74½ x 55½ inches (189.2 x 141 cm)
Cotton fabric, cotton thread, cotton batting; machine quilted, pieced
QUILTED BY SUE DIVARCO
PHOTO BY PAUL LANE

LAWNA L. COLLINS
It's A Mystery ■ 2010
104 x 88 inches (264.2 x 223.5 cm)
Cotton fabric, cotton thread, cotton batting; machine pieced, machine quilted
QUILTED BY CAROLE ANN GARDNER
PHOTO BY NATHANIEL & DIAN MASSEY

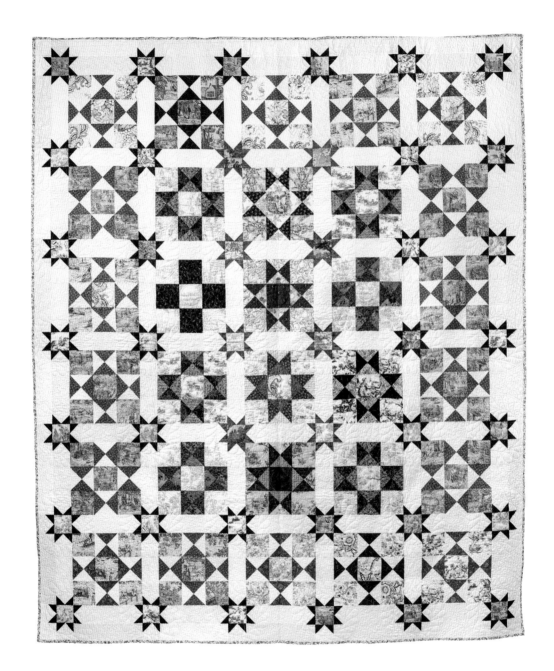

VIVIAN HELENA AUMOND-CAPONE
Variable Toile Stars ■ 2004
98½ x 83½ inches (250.2 x 212.1 cm)
Toile fabrics; long-arm machine quilted
QUILTED BY SHIRLEY GREENHOE
PHOTO BY ARTIST

**MELBA DRENNAN, WINNIE FLEMING, MARCIA BRENNER,
BEVERLY FRENCH, DEBBIE BROWN, PAMELA FERNANDEZ**
Feathered by Friends ■ 2012–2013
90 x 72 inches (228.6 x 182.9 cm)
Cotton fabric, thread; pieced
PHOTO BY MEG MCKINNEY

321

GINGER QUINN MUÑOZ
The Stars in the Garden ■ 2005
62³/₄ x 50³/₄ inches (159.4 x 128.9 cm)
Cotton fabric, cotton and nylon thread,
cotton batting; machine quilted
PHOTO BY ARTIST

SUSAN STEWART
Radiance ■ 2011
74 x 75 inches (188 x 190.5 cm)
Pieced, machine embroidered, machine
stitched, free-motion machine quilted
PHOTO BY ARTIST

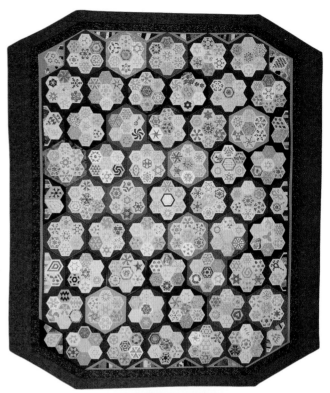

ARDIE SKJOD
Star Garden ■ 2010
80 x 72 inches (203.2 x 182.9 cm)
Cotton reproductions, cotton thread, cotton
batting; machine pieced, machine quilted
PHOTO BY DEBBIE BLAIR

CINZIA WHITE
Raconteuer – The Storyteller's Collection ■ 2006–2012
106 x 91 inches (269.2 x 231.1 cm)
Cotton fabric, cotton thread, wool/polyester batting;
machine quilted, hand and machine pieced, hand
embroidered, hand and machine appliquéd
PHOTOS BY DAVIS JAMES

ISAKO WADA
Bolero 21609 ■ 2010

101 x 88 inches (256.5 x 223.5 cm)
Cotton fabric, polyester thread, polyester
batting; hand quilted, hand pieced
PHOTO BY ARTIST

COLEEN THACKRAY
Still a Mystery ■ 2011
61 x 61 inches (154.9 x 154.9 cm)
Cotton fabric, cotton thread, cotton/polyester
batting; hand quilted, machine pieced
PHOTO BY MALCOLM THACKRAY

HOLLY SWEET
Kaleidoscope Rhapsody ■ 1996
64 x 52½ inches (162.6 x 133.4 cm)
Cotton fabric, cotton and metallic thread, cotton/polyester
batting; machine quilted, hand and machine pieced
PHOTO BY MAGGIE WILSON

SUSAN CATANZARITO
Feathered Star ■ 2005

62 x 62 inches (157.5 x 157.5 cm)
Cotton fabrics, Civil War reproductions; paper pieced,
machine pieced, needle-turn appliquéd, machine quilted
QUILTED BY LINDA MCCUEAN
PHOTO BY TIM HUFF

327

CONNIE WATKINS
Sunburst ◼ 2012
75 x 75 inches (190.5 x 190.5 cm)
Cotton fabric, cotton thread, wool
batting; hand quilted, hand appliquéd
PHOTO BY MIKE MCCORMICK

LORI SCHMITT ALLISON
Mariner's Compass ■ 2008
47 x 47 inches (119.4 x 119.4 cm)
Cotton fabric, cotton thread, cotton
batting; hand pieced, hand quilted
PHOTO BY GREGORY CASE PHOTOGRAPHY

GEORGANN WRINKLE
Dear Jane Goes Around the Block ■ 2012
64 x 64 inches (162.6 x 162.6 cm)
Cotton fabric, cotton thread, wool batting;
machine quilted, machine pieced
QUILTED BY DENISE GREEN
PHOTO BY JULIE PAPPAN

RAHNA WALKER SUMMERLIN
Blooming in Chintz ■ 2006
90 x 110 inches (228.6 x 279.4 cm)
Cotton fabrics, cotton thread,
80/20 cotton/polyester batting;
machine pieced, machine quilted
PHOTOS BY ARTIST

MARILYN BADGER
Big Bird Blues ■ 2007
86 x 86 inches (218.4 x 218.4 cm)
Cotton fabric, polyester thread, cotton batting;
machine pieced, machine appliquéd, machine quilted
DESIGNED AND PIECED BY CLAUDIA CLARK MYERS
PHOTO BY CLAUDIA CLARK MYERS

331

VICKI CULVER ANDERSON
Lone Star Pride and Joy ■ 2012
101 x 101 inches (256.5 x 256.5 cm)
Cotton fabric, cotton thread, cotton
batting; pieced, machine quilted
QUILTED BY JULIA MASON
PHOTO BY PAMELA FULCHER

KATHLEEN ERBECK
Grandma's Inspiration ■ 2004
90 x 82 inches (228.6 x 208.3 cm)
Cotton fabric, cotton batting;
machine pieced, machine quilted
PHOTO BY SANDRA WOJTAL WEBER

ROUND ROBIN GROUP-WINNIE FLEMING, PAMELA FERNANDEZ, MARCIA BRENNER, BEVERLY FRENCH, MELBA DRENNAN
Chocolate & Cherries ■ 2008-2009
80 x 80 inches (203.2 x 203.2 cm)
Cotton Civil War reproduction fabric, cotton thread; machine quilted
QUILTED BY DENISE GREEN
PHOTO BY JIM & JUDY LINCOLN

FACING PAGE **CHRISTINE N. BROWN**
Feathered Dreams ■ 2003

72 x 59½ inches (182.9 x 151.1 cm)
Cotton fabric, cotton thread, cotton batting;
machine pieced, hand appliquéd, hand quilted
BLOCK DESIGN BY DIANA PETTERSON
PHOTO BY CHARLES R. LYNCH

FAYE ANDERSON
Xanadu ■ 1993

80 x 60 inches (203.2 x 152.4 cm)
Cotton fabric, cotton thread, cotton
batting; hand quilted, appliquéd, pieced
PHOTO BY KEN SAMVILLE

REBECCA ROHRKASTE
Cross Between ◼ 1989
79 x 79 inches (200.7 x 200.7 cm)
Cotton fabric, cotton thread, cotton/polyester
batting; hand quilted, machine pieced
PHOTO BY SHARON RISEDORPH

ANN J. HARWELL
Starry, Starry Knightdale ■ 1991

94 x 72 inches (238.8 x 182.9 cm)
Cotton fabric, cotton thread,
cotton batting; hand quilted
PHOTO BY LYNN RUCK

337

NANCY C. ARSENEAULT
Time to Do It! ■ 2010
76 x 76 inches (193 x 193 cm)
Cotton fabric, cotton thread, wool batting;
machine pieced, machine quilted
PHOTO BY INTERNATIONAL QUILT ASSOCIATION

CLAUDIA CLARK MYERS
Mediterranean Beauty ■ 2002

90 x 90 inches (228.6 x 228.6 cm)
Hand-dyed cotton fabric, polyester thread, 80/20 batting;
long-arm machine quilted, machine pieced
QUILTED BY MARILYN BADGER
PHOTO BY JEFF FREY

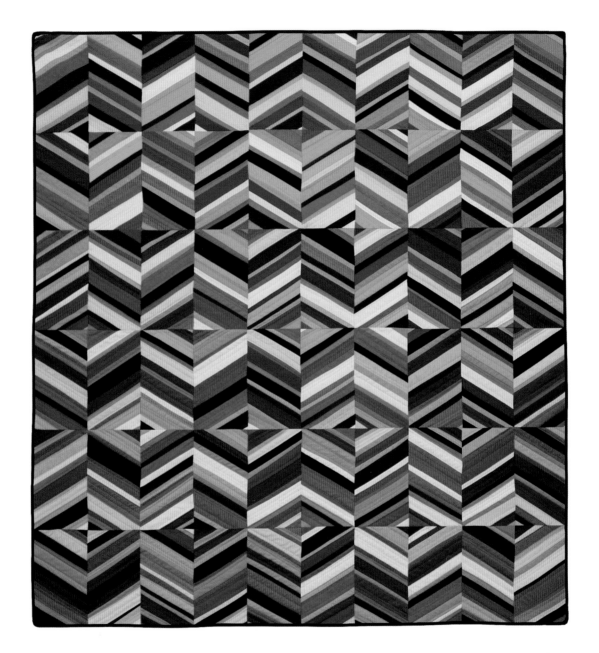

TARA FAUGHNAN
Alexandra's Quilt ■ 2012
58 x 55 inches (147.3 x 139.7 cm)
Cotton fabrics, cotton thread;
machine pieced and quilted
PHOTO BY ARTIST

FACING PAGE **CHRIS SERONG**
Joseph's Coat with Buttons ■ 2010
88 x 73 inches (223.5 x 185.4 x cm)
Cotton fabric, cotton thread, wool batting;
hand pieced, hand appliquéd, machine quilted
QUILTED BY SUSAN CAMPBELL
PHOTO BY ARTIST

341

JOYCE LYON SAIA
Logs and Leaves ■ 2009
80 x 80 inches (203.2 x 203.2 cm)
Hand-dyed cotton fabric, cotton batting;
machine appliquéd and embroidered
PHOTO BY INTERNATIONAL QUILT ASSOCIATION

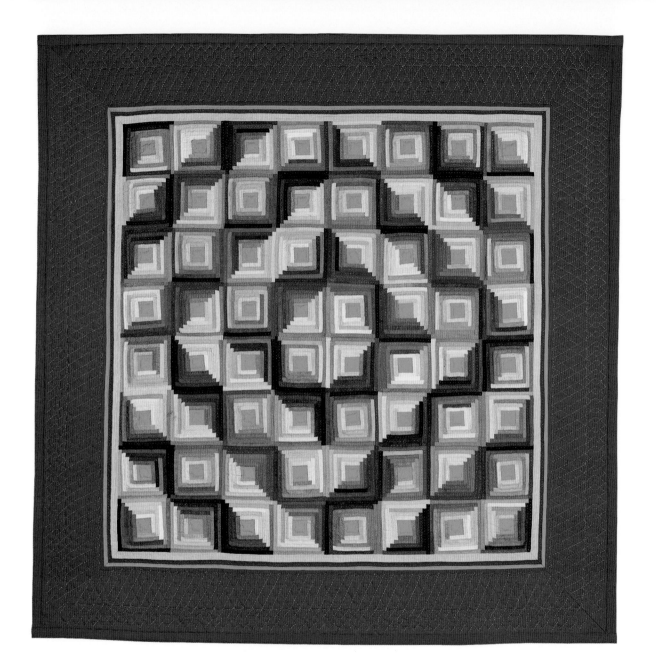

GRETCHEN NEAL JACKSON
Little Logs ■ 2008

38 x 38 inches (96.5 x 96.5 cm)
Hand-dyed solid cotton fabrics; machine
pieced, hand embroidered, hand quilted
PHOTO BY ERIC LAWS

FACING PAGE **ANITA GROSSMAN SOLOMON**
Self-Mitered Log Cabin ■ 2008
81 x 69 inches (205.7 x 175.3 cm)
Cotton fabric, cotton thread, cotton batting; machine quilted, pieced
QUILTED BY JANICE E. PETRE
PHOTO BY CHRISTINA CARTY-FRANCIS & DIANE PEDERSON

DIANA FAWN SHARKEY
First Ladies Log Cabin ■ 2011
52 x 52 inches (132.1 x 132.1 cm)
Cotton fabrics, cotton thread, cotton batting
PHOTO BY HOWARD GOODMAN

345

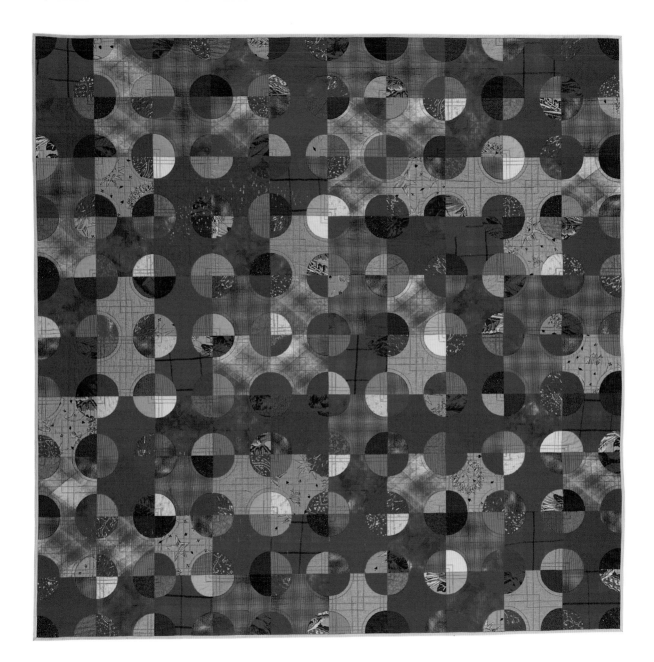

REBECCA ROHRKASTE
Full Circle ■ 2000
80 x 80 inches (203.2 x 203.2 cm)
Cotton fabric, cotton thread, cotton batting;
machine pieced, machine quilted
PHOTO BY DAVID BELDA

CINDY GRISDELA
Playing with Crayons ■ 2006

56 x 56 inches (142.2 x 142.2 cm)
Cotton batik fabric, cotton variegated thread,
cotton batting; machine quilted, pieced
PHOTO BY GREGORY STALEY

KEIKO GOKE
My Double Wedding Ring ■ 2008
88 x 86 inches (223.5 x 218.4 cm)
Cotton fabrics; machine pieced, quilted
PHOTO BY ARTIST

SUSAN DAGUE
Dot to Dot ■ 2006
83 x 74 inches (210.8 x 188 cm)
Cotton fabric, cotton thread,
cotton batting; pieced
PHOTO BY SIBILA SAVAGE

KEIKO GOKE
My Basket ■ 2008
88 x 75 inches (223.5 x 190.5 cm)
Cotton fabrics; machine pieced, quilted
PHOTO BY ARTIST

JANET HAYDAY
New York Beauty ■ 2009
51 x 51 inches (129.5 x 129.5 cm)
Cotton fabric and batting; machine quilted
PHOTO BY TERON ANSCOMBE

ANN T. PIGNERI
Hope ■ 2010

74 inches (188 cm) in diameter
Cotton fabric, polyester and metallic threads, crystals, wool batting;
free-motion machine quilted, hand appliquéd, machine pieced
PHOTO BY GREGORY CASE

DIANE BECKA
Almost Amish Baskets ■ 2000
15 x 15 inches (38.1 x 38.1 cm)
Cotton fabric, cotton thread, cotton batting;
machine pieced, hand appliquéd, machine quilted
PHOTO BY ARTIST

SHIRLEY FOWLKES STEVENSON
Night Shade ■ 2013

67 x 67 inches (170.2 x 170.2 cm)
Cotton fabrics, thread, batting; machine pieced,
appliquéd, quilted, hand embroidered
QUILTED BY RICHARD LARSON
PHOTO BY ARTIST

353

CHERYL SEE
Star Struck ■ 2011
80 x 91 inches (203.2 x 231.1 cm)
Cotton fabric, cotton thread, assorted beads; English
paper pieced, appliquéd, hand embroidered, hand
quilted, hand beaded, watercolor technique
PHOTO BY KIM COUGHLIN

CINDY GRISDELA
Playing with Colors ■ 2008
45 x 54 inches (114.3 x 137.2 cm)
Cotton batik fabric, cotton variegated thread,
cotton batting; machine quilted, pieced
PHOTO BY GREGORY STALEY

355

JANET HAYDAY
Color Pyramids ■ 2012
74 x 54 inches (188 x 137.2 cm)
Cotton fabrics, batting and thread; machine pieced and quilted
QUILTED BY JANICE JAMISON
PHOTO BY TERON ANSCOMBE

MARVA M. SWANSON
Tumbling in Space ■ 2009
82 x 60 inches (208.3 x 152.4 cm)
Hand-dyed fabrics; hand appliquéd
QUILTED BY REGINA CARTER
PHOTO BY ARTIST

GINGER QUINN MUÑOZ
High Country Garden ■ 1999
67¼ x 55 inches (170.8 x 139.7 cm)
Cotton fabric, cotton and nylon thread,
polyester batting; machine quilted
PHOTO BY ARTIST

357

V'LOU OLIVEIRA
Crazy Stars ■ 2009
57½ x 47 inches (146.1 x 119.4 cm)
Cotton fabrics, cotton thread, cotton
batting; machine pieced, machine quilted
PHOTO BY ED HATCH

IRENE MCGUIRE ANDREWS
Flower Girls ■ 2007
69 x 69 inches (175.3 x 175.3 cm)
Cotton fabric, cotton thread, cotton/polyester
batting; hand appliquéd, hand quilted
PHOTO BY STEVE SULLIVAN

CINZIA WHITE
Turkish Delight ▦ 2010
96½ x 96½ inches (245.1 x 245.1 cm)
Cotton fabric, cotton thread, wool/polyester batting;
hand appliquéd, machine pieced, machine quilted
QUILTED BY MAXINE SANDRY AND CINZIA WHITE
PHOTO BY ANTHONY BURNS

BETSY CHUTCHIAN
Almost 1000 Pyramids ■ 2003–2008

58 x 47 inches (147.3 x 119.4 cm)
Cotton fabric, cotton thread, cotton batting;
machine pieced and qulited
QUILTED BY SHERI MECOM
PHOTO BY ANNETTE PLOG

JUDY E. MARTIN
Flesh and Blood ■ 2003
90 x 90 inches (228.6 x 228.6 cm)
Cotton batting, dye, silk fabric, cotton fabric, polyester sheer fabric,
buttons; hand quilted, appliquéd, embroidered, pieced
PHOTOS BY SARAH WARBURTON

PAM HILL
Under Southern Skies ■ 2009
96 x 96 inches (243.8 x 243.8 cm)
Cotton fabric, cotton batting, cotton and
silk thread; machine pieced and quilted
PHOTO BY JULIEN STAR

361

HOLLY SWEET
Red Squares & Rectangles ■ 2004
86½ x 66 inches (219.7 x 167.6 cm)
Cotton fabric, cotton and perle cotton thread,
polyester batting; hand quilted, machine pieced
PHOTO BY MAGGIE WILSON

FACING PAGE **SUSAN DAGUE**
Redwork Revisited ■ 2011
89 x 71 inches (226.1 x 180.3 cm)
Cotton fabric, cotton batting, cotton thread and floss;
hand embroidered, hand and machine quilted, machine pieced
PHOTO BY SIBILA SAVAGE

500
traditional quilts

363

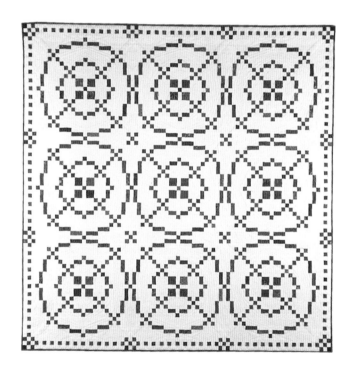

JANICE KEENE MADDOX
Trellis of Roses ■ 2002
77 x 77 inches (195.6 x 195.6 cm)
Cotton fabrics, rayon threads, cotton batting;
machine pieced and quilted, machine trapunto
PHOTO BY TIM BARNWELL

PAT CONNALLY
Stars All Around ■ 2006
89 x 89 inches (226.1 x 226.1 cm)
Cotton fabric, cotton thread; machine
pieced, long-arm machine quilted
PHOTO BY JIM & JUDY LINCOLN

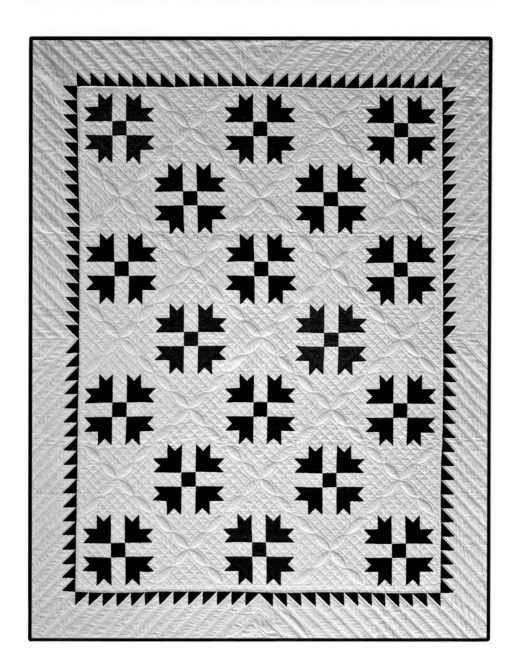

MINAY SIROIS
Cross and Crown ■ 2003
85 x 65 inches (215.9 x 165.1 cm)
Cotton fabric, cotton thread, cotton batting;
machine pieced, hand quilted, trapunto
PHOTO BY MICHAEL SIROIS

365

ANNETTE M. BURGESS
President's Wreath ■ 2011
7 3/8 x 7 3/8 inches (18.7 x 18.7 cm)
Cotton fabrics, cotton/polyester and silk threads,
80/20 cotton/polyester batting; machine
pieced, hand appliquéd, machine quilted
PHOTO BY ARTIST

SCARLETT ROSE
Celtic Medallion II ■ 1992
40 x 40 inches (101.6 x 101.6 cm)
Cotton fabric, tricot lame fabric, cotton thread, polyester
batting; hand quilted, machine quilted, hand appliquéd
PHOTO BY HARVEY J. SPECTOR

CAROLE J. DUNKLAU

Roses Are Red ■ 1996

86 x 86 inches (218.4 x 218.4 cm)
Cotton fabric, cotton thread, polyester batting;
hand appliquéd, hand quilted

QUILTED BY CAROL WURTH
DESIGN BY MURIEL DOUGLAS AND PATTY MILLER
PHOTO BY ARTIST

367

DAWN FOX COOPER
Kootenay Peony ■ 2012
45 x 45 inches (114.3 x 114.3 cm)
Cotton fabric, polyester fabric, polyester wired ribbon,
bamboo/cotton batting; hand quilted, hand appliquéd,
ruched, padded appliquéd, machine pieced
PHOTO BY ARTIST

JERRIANNE EVANS
Borrowed Roses ■ 2012
85 x 85 inches (215.9 x 215.9 cm)
Cotton fabric, silk batting; hand appliquéd,
machine pieced, machine quilted
QUILTED BY CYNTHIA CLARK, PATTERN BY SUE GARMAN
PHOTO BY JAMES EVANS

RITA VERROCA
Sun-Dance Quilt ■ 2003
106 x 82 inches (269.2 x 208.3 cm)
Cotton fabric, cotton thread, cotton batting;
hand appliquéd, hand quilted, hand pieced
PHOTO BY STEVIE VERROCA

369

GEORGANN WRINKLE
Little Lily ■ 2012
35 x 35 inches (88.9 x 88.9 cm)
Cotton fabric, cotton thread, wool
batting; hand appliquéd, hand quilted
PHOTO BY JULIE PAPPAN

WEN REDMOND
First and Last Star ■ 1984
45 x 45 inches (114.3 x 114.3 cm)
Cotton fabrics, cotton thread, cotton batting;
hand quilted, 3D appliquéd, pieced
PHOTO BY ARTIST

LAURIE MAYO
Flocks of Geese ■ 2012

85 x 88½ inches (215.9 x 224.8 cm)
Cotton fabric, cotton and polyester thread, cotton batting; hand and machine pieced, hand quilted

PIECED BY LAURIE MAYO, ROSA BONILLA, MARYVANN ESLINGER, GWEN GOEPEL, GERRI HIRASAWA, PEGGY JONES, LILLIAN LAWRENCE, GEORGIA LENINS, CAITLIN MAYO, PUDGE MCCUTCHEON, GRETCHEN MONROE, TABBIE NANCE, DIANNA VACCARELLA, EILEEN WILLIAMS
QUILTED BY LAURIE MAYO, MARY ANN FRENCH, KAREN HART, GERRI HIRASAWA, PAULA JOHNSON, ELIZABETH MCCORMICK, VALERIE MILLIMAN, GRETCHEN MONROE, PINKY PORTER, KAREN ZAENKER
PHOTO BY GREGORY CASE PHOTOGRAPHY

371

JANE BERGSTRALH
Dan's Baltimore Album ■ 2006

88 x 88 inches (223.5 x 223.5 cm)
Cotton fabric, cotton thread, cotton batting;
hand quilted, hand appliquéd
PHOTO BY CRAIG MCDOUGAL

SANDRA L. MOLLON
Frederick County Album ■ 1992–1994

82 x 82 inches (208.3 x 208.3 cm)
Cotton fabric, cotton threads, cotton batting;
hand quilted, hand appliquéd, machine pieced
PHOTO BY ARTIST

373

LAHALA PHELPS
Love Never Ends ■ 2003
92 x 92 inches (233.7 x 233.7 cm)
Cotton fabric, cotton thread, polyester batting;
hand quilted, hand appliquéd
PHOTO BY MARK FREY

SANDIE LUSH
Tulips ■ 2003
79½ x 81 inches (201.9 x 205.7 cm)
Cotton fabric, cotton thread, wool batting; machine
pieced, hand appliquéd, hand quilted
PHOTO BY DAVID LUSH

KAREN PESSIA
My Baltimore Journey ■ 2008
68 x 68 inches (172.7 x 172.7 cm)
Cotton fabrics, ultrasuede, cotton and silk threads,
embroidery floss, cotton batting; hand appliquéd,
embroidered, machine pieced, hand quilted
PHOTO BY JEFFREY LOMICKA

MARY ELLEN G. SPAHR
Whig Rose Revisited ■ 2011
98 x 98 inches (248.9 x 248.9 cm)
Cotton fabric, cotton thread, cotton batting;
free-hand machine quilted, appliquéd and pieced
QUILTED BY BOBBIE LEHMAN
PHOTO BY WES GRADY

FACING PAGE **JANE HALL**
Princess Feather and Rising Star ■ 1990
87 x 70 inches (221 x 177.8 cm)
Cotton fabric, cotton thread, polyester batting;
hand and machine pieced, hand appliquéd, hand quilted
IN COLLABORATION WITH MARTHA BATTLE, JEAN DAVIES, MARY GEIGER, NANCY GREEN, PAT
PATTERSON, KATHY SULLIVAN, AILEEN TARVER, ANNE WEAVER, GERRY WINSTEAD
PHOTO BY RICHARD COX

377

DAWN FOX COOPER
Kootenay Rose ■ 2012
40 x 40 inches (101.6 x 101.6 cm)
Cotton fabric, polyester satin ribbon, brocade; machine
pieced, hand appliquéd, ruched, hand quilted
PHOTO BY ARTIST

JOANN HANNAH
Cherry Basket ■ 1999
72 x 72 inches (182.9 x 182.9 cm)
Cotton fabric, cotton thread, cotton batting;
hand quilted, hand appliquéd, trapunto
PHOTO BY JIM & JUDY LINCOLN

RITA VERROCA
Prairie Trails ■ 2006
98 x 98 inches (248.9 x 248.9 cm)
Cotton fabric, cotton thread, cotton batting;
hand appliquéd, hand quilted, hand pieced
PHOTO BY STEVIE VERROCA

379

DARLENE DONOHUE
Red and Green Revisited ■ 2011
82 x 84 inches (208.3 x 213.4 cm)
Cotton reproduction fabric, silk thread, cotton batting;
hand appliquéd, machine quilted
QUILTED BY DEBBIE YEZBAK
PHOTO BY CYNTHIA MCINTYRE

ZENA THORPE
Crowned with Glory – Right Royally ■ 1996

89 x 86 inches (226.1 x 218.4 cm)
Cotton fabric, lame, cotton batting;
hand quilted, hand appliquéd
PHOTO BY DONALD LEVINE

LEIGH ELKING
Autumn Rhapsody ■ 2006
18 x 18 inches (45.7 x 45.7 cm)
Batik fabric, cotton, silk and metallic thread, batting;
hand and machine appliquéd, machine quilted
PHOTO BY ARTIST

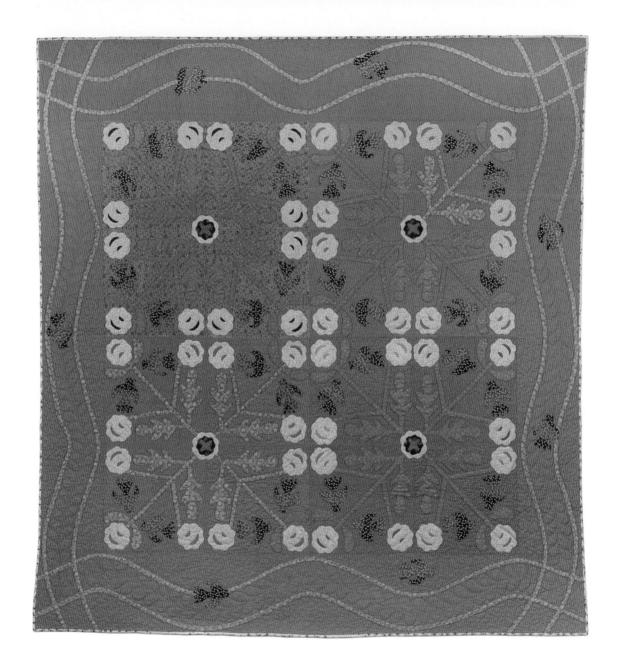

MICKEY BEEBE

Yellow Roses and Blue Birds | 2006

82 x 78 inches (208.3 x 198.1 cm)
Cotton fabric, 80/20 batting; hand-guided
machine quilted, machine appliquéd, pieced
QUILTED BY MARY LUNDBERG
PHOTO BY ALAN PORTER

383

PAT PETERS
Irish Summer Garden ■ 2012
105 x 105 inches (266.7 x 266.7 cm)
Cotton batiks, silk thread, polyester batting,
cotton thread; appliquéd, hand quilted
PHOTO BY SHAUNA STEPHENSON

KEIKO MIYAUCHI
A Present of Roses ■ 2003
83 ³/₄ x 76 ³/₄ inches (212.7 x 194.9 cm)
Cotton fabric, polyester thread, polyester batting;
hand quilted, hand appliquéd, trapunto

BARBARA ANN MCCRAW
Out of Africa ■ 2012

85 x 85 inches (215.9 x 215.9 cm)
Cotton fabric, thread, 80/20 batting; machine
appliquéd, machine pieced, machine quilted

LESLIE KIGER
Covington Medallions ■ 2009

85 x 85 inches (215.9 x 215.9 cm)
Batik fabrics, cotton thread, 80/20
batting; machine pieced, machine quilted
QUILTED BY JOAN KNIGHT
PHOTO BY ARTIST

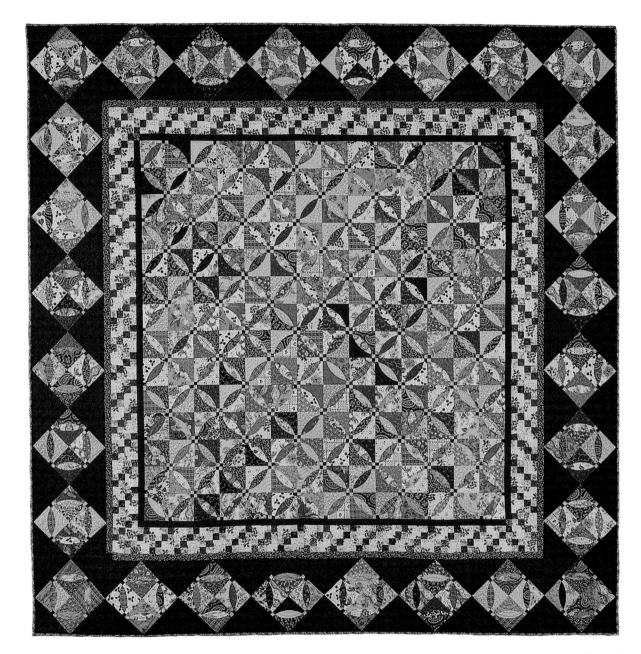

MARGARET MCDONALD
Entwined ■ 2007
90 x 90 inches (228.6 x 228.6 cm)
Cotton fabric, cotton thread, cotton batting;
long-arm machine quilted, pieced
QUILTED BY SUSAN CAMPBELL
PHOTO BY J. CHRIS MCDONALD

FACING PAGE **NORIKO KIDO**
Promise ■ 2005
85 x 74½ inches (215.9 x 189.2 cm)
Cotton fabric, cotton and polyester
thread, polyester batting; hand quilted,
appliquéd, pieced, embroidered
PHOTO BY AKINORI MIYASHITA

389

FACING PAGE **TIMNA TARR**
Portraits of Flora ■ 2011
58 x 51 inches (147.3 x 129.5 cm)
Cotton fabric, cotton thread, wool batting;
machine quilted, hand appliquéd, machine pieced
PHOTO BY STEPHEN PETEGORSKY

HELEN REMICK
In Honor of the Marriage of Elizabeth and Yuki ■ 2006
72 x 60 inches (182.9 x 152.4 cm)
Cotton fabric, cotton thread, cotton batting, gold trim;
hand pieced, appliquéd, and quilted, hand couched
PHOTO BY MARK FREY

BONNIE RAYE KUCERA
Birds in the Rafters ◾ 2004
94 x 90 inches (238.8 x 228.6 cm)
Cotton fabric, cotton thread; hand quilted, hand appliquéd,
hand and machine embroidered, machine pieced
PHOTO BY ARTIST

NANCY S. BROWN
Great Grandpa Brown ▪ 2002

24 x 20 inches (61 x 50.8 cm)
Cotton fabric, cotton thread, 80/20 batting;
hand quilted, hand appliquéd, machine pieced
PHOTO BY ARTIST

393

V'LOU OLIVEIRA
Red Crazy Stars ■ 2010
56½ x 45 inches (146.1 x 114.3 cm)
Cotton fabrics, cotton thread, cotton batting;
machine pieced, machine quilted
PHOTO BY ED HATCH

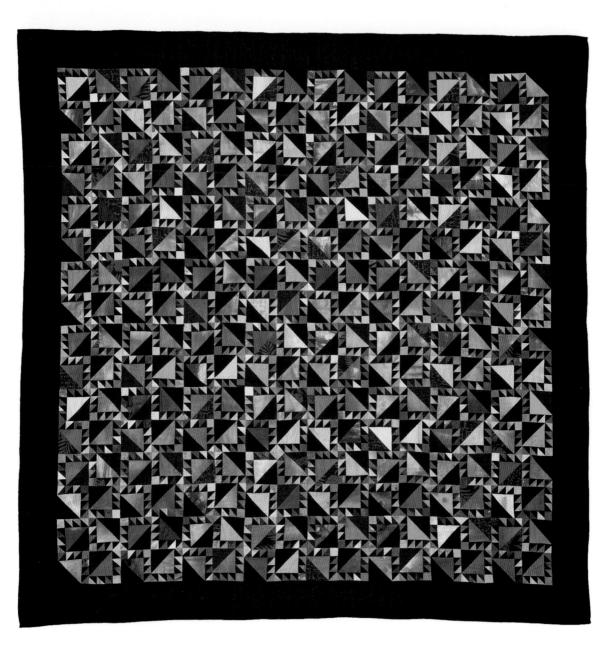

SARAH ALBRIGHT DICKSON
Untitled ■ 1998

79 x 79 inches (200.7 x 200.7 cm)
Cotton fabric, cotton thread, hand-dyed
fabrics; machine pieced, hand quilted
PHOTO BY JIM & JUDY LINCOLN

ANNE-MARIE UGUEN
Framed Medallion ■ 2009
78 ¾ x 78 ¾ inches (200 x 200 cm)
Cotton fabric, cotton thread, cotton batting; hand pieced
PHOTO BY FRANCE PATCHWORK

LYNN B. WELSCH
Texas Triumph ■ 1992
106 x 97 inches (269.2 x 246.4 cm)
Cotton fabric, cotton and nylon thread, 80/20 cotton batting;
machine piece, machine appliquéd
PHOTO BY JIM & JUDY LINCOLN

397

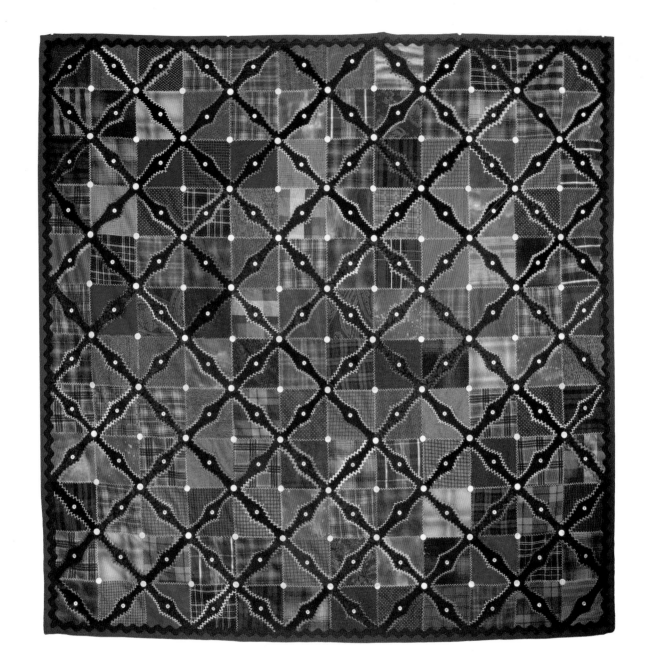

ALLISON ALLER
Crazy for Plaid ■ 2012
72 x 72 inches (182.9 x 182.9 cm)
Wool, silk, and cotton fabrics, silk ribbon, cotton batting, buttons;
hand and machine embroidered, appliquéd, pieced, tied
PHOTO BY INTERNATIONAL QUILT ASSOCIATION

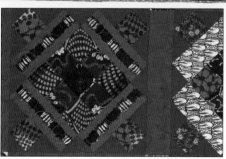

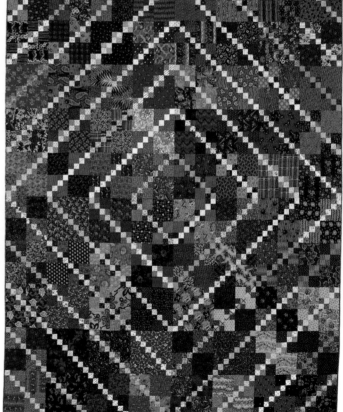

MICKEY BEEBE
Country Barter ■ 2008
90 x 66 inches (228.6 x 167.6 cm)
African fabric, Japanese fabric, 80/20 batting;
hand-guided machine quilted, pieced
QUILTED BY MARY LUNDBERG
PHOTOS BY ALAN PORTER

MARILYN WARD MOWRY
Triple Four Patch ■ 2007
80 x 64 inches (203.2 x 162.6 cm)
Cotton reproduction fabrics, cotton thread, cotton
batting; machine pieced, machine quilted
QUILTED BY SHERI MECOM
PHOTO BY ARTIST

PATRICIA T. MAYER
Tribute to Jane ■ 2008
81 x 81 inches (205.7 x 205.7 cm)
Cotton fabric, cotton thread, cotton batting;
hand pieced, hand appliquéd, machine quilted
QUILTED BY KAREN WATTS
PHOTO BY INTERNATIONAL QUILT ASSOCIATION

CAROL STAEHLE

Salute to Salinda ■ 2005

88 x 88 inches (223.5 x 223.5 cm)
Cotton fabrics; foundation paper
pieced, machine quilted

PHOTO BY ANNETTE PLOG

401

YOSHIKO KOBAYASHI
Ancient Mirror Came from Across the Sea ■ 1999
60¼ x 60¼ inches (153 x 153 cm)
Cotton fabric, cotton thread, polyester batting;
hand quilted, machine pieced
PHOTO BY SUN PHOTO STUDIO

500
traditional quilts

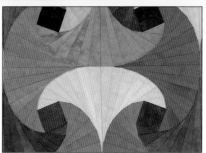

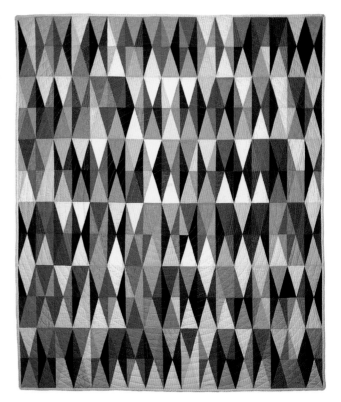

BRIGITTE MORGENROTH
Opernball ■ 2005
85 ³/₄ x 62 ¹/₄ inches (217.8 x 158.1 cm)
Hand-dyed cotton, polyester thread, polyester
batting; hand quilted, paper pieced
PHOTOS BY ALBRECHT MORGENROTH

TARA FAUGHNAN
Diamonds Quilt ■ 2012
54 x 46 inches (137.2 x 116.8 cm)
Cotton, cotton/polyester blends, linen, cotton
thread and batting; machine pieced and quilted
PHOTO BY ARTIST

403

CHRIS SERONG
Sunflowers ■ 2008
73 x 73 inches (185.4 x 185.4 cm)
Cotton fabric, cotton thread, wool batting; foundation
pieced, reverse appliquéd, machine pieced, machine quilted

QUILTED BY SUSAN CAMPBELL
PHOTO BY ARTIST

FACING PAGE **ANNIE MOODY,
LYNDA REMMERS, SHARON SCHAMBER**
Feathered Star ■ 2012
108 x 93 inches (274.3 x 236.2 cm)
Batting; pieced, quilted in the hoop

DESIGN BY HOOPSISTERS.COM
PHOTO BY XPRESSIONS BY HEATHER ALLISON

405

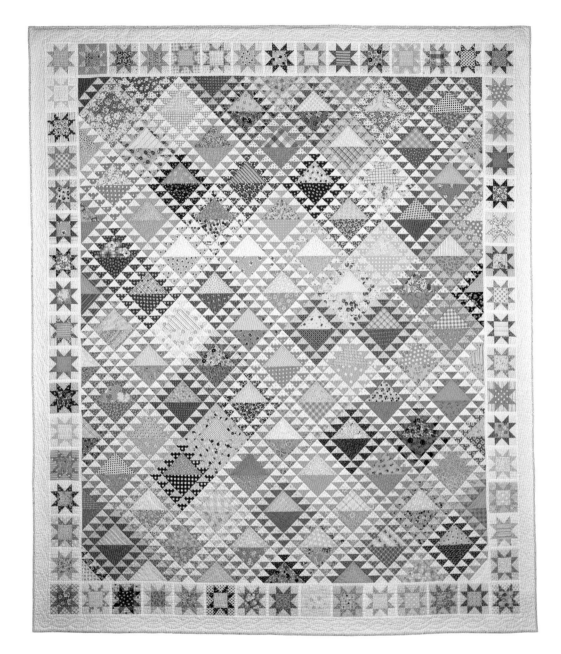

RAHNA WALKER SUMMERLIN
Summer at the Lake ■ 2010
86 x 75 inches (218.4 x 190.5 cm)
Cotton fabrics, cotton thread, 80/20 cotton/
polyester batting; machine pieced, machine quilted
PHOTO BY DAVID ELMQUIST

500
traditional quilts

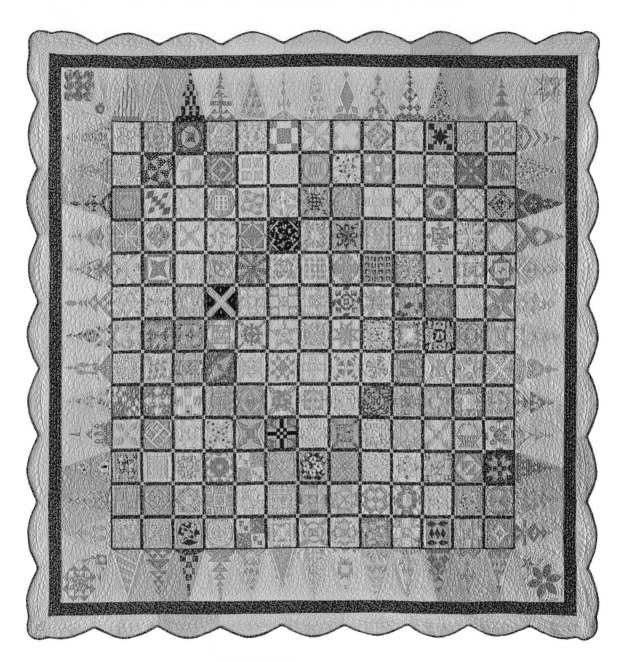

CINDY GARCIA
No Pain, No Jane ■ 2007
88 x 88 inches (223.5 x 223.5 cm)
Cotton fabrics, cotton and rayon
threads, cotton batting; hand appliquéd,
machine pieced, machine quilted
PHOTO BY GREGORY CASE PHOTOGRAPHY

WENDY HILL
Daisy Doodle ■ 2008
97 x 86 inches (246.4 x 218.4 cm)
Reproduction cotton fabrics; self-made
bias-covered curves, machine quilted
PHOTO BY CRAIG HOWELL

DAWN FOX COOPER

Single Wedding Ring ■ 2011

87 x 84 inches (221 x 213.4 cm)
Cotton fabric, cotton polyester thread, bamboo
and cotton batting; hand pieced, hand quilted
PHOTO BY MICHAEL MAYRHOFER

409

LINDA STEELE
Holiday Waltz ■ 2012
78½ x 77¼ inches (199.4 x 196.2 cm)
Cotton fabric, silk thread, wool batting;
machine quilted, hand appliquéd, trapunto
PHOTO BY ARTIST

YACHIYO KATSUNO
Sunshine Rose Garden ■ 2003
91 x 90 inches (231.1 x 228.6 cm)
Cotton fabric, polyester thread, polyester batting;
hand pieced, hand quilted

MICHELE A. BARNES
Texas Hay Rake ■ 2009
94 x 94 inches (238.8 x 238.8 cm)
Cotton fabric, cotton thread, silk batting;
hand quilted, hand appliquéd
PHOTO BY PHIL BARNES

413

MARGARET MCDONALD
Amazed ■ 2011
64 1/2 x 64 1/2 inches (163.8 x 163.8 cm)
Cotton fabric, cotton thread, wool/polyester
batting; long-arm machine quilted, pieced

QUILTED BY SUSAN CAMPBELL
COLLECTION OF CENTRAL GOLDFIELDS ART GALLERY, VICTORIA, AUSTRALIA
PHOTO BY J. CHRIS MCDONALD

PATRICIA L. DELANEY
To Everything There Is a Season ■ 2010

84 x 84 inches (213.4 x 213.4 cm)
Cotton fabric, cotton thread, rayon thread, silk batting;
machine paper pieced, machine quilted, machine
embroidered, machine appliquéd, hand couched
PHOTO BY MATTHEW DELANEY

415

BETTY CAWTHON DAY
Never Again New York Beauty ■ 2005
84 x 84 inches (213.4 x 213.4 cm)
Cotton fabric, cotton thread, cotton batting; hand
quilted, appliquéd, machine pieced, trapunto
PHOTO BY ALLEN DAY

RITA VERROCA
Roses of Shenandoah ■ 2010

86 x 86 inches (218.4 x 218.4 cm)
Cotton fabric, cotton thread, cotton batting;
hand appliquéd, hand quilted, hand pieced
PHOTO BY STEVIE VERROCA

MARLINE TURNER
Passion Lives on Jess ■ 2006
86 x 86 inches (218.4 x 218.4 cm)
Cotton fabric, silk thread, batting;
hand quilted, hand appliquéd
PHOTO BY ARTIST

SCARLETT ROSE
A Celtic Rose Garden ■ 2001
50 x 50 inches (127 x 127 cm)
Cotton fabric, tricot lame fabric, cotton thread, rayon thread,
metallic thread, polyester batting; machine quilted,
hand quilted, hand appliquéd, machine pieced
PHOTO BY HARVEY J. SPECTOR

CAROLE J. DUNKLAU
Wisconsin Wedding Quilt ■ 2007

76 x 69 inches (193 x 175.3 cm)
Cotton fabric, cotton thread, polyester
batting; hand quilted, appliquéd, pieced

QUILTED BY CAROL WURTH
PHOTO BY ARTIST

419

JOANN HANNAH
Hannah's Garden ■ 1997
82 x 82 inches (208.3 x 208.3 cm)
Cotton fabric, cotton thread, cotton batting;
hand quilted, appliquéd
PHOTO BY JIM & JUDY LINCOLN

TED STORM

Nocturnal Garden ■ 2001

80 x 80 inches (203.2 x 203.2 cm)
Cotton and silk fabrics, cotton thread, perle cotton thread, Shisha mirrors, 80/20 cotton/polyester
batting; hand appliquéd, padded appliquéd, embroidered, machine pieced, hand quilted
PHOTO BY JIM & JUDY LINCOLN

421

KEIKO MIYAUCHI
Flowers in Taj Mahal ■ 2006
91¼ x 87⅓ inches (231.8 x 221.8 cm)
Cotton fabric, polyester thread, polyester batting;
hand quilted, hand appliquéd, trapunto
PHOTO BY NORIAKI MORIYA

ZENA THORPE

Kells: Magnum Opus ■ 2001

92 x 82 inches (233.7 x 208.3 cm)
Cotton fabric, cotton thread, cotton batting;
hand quilted, hand appliquéd
PHOTO BY DONALD LEVINE

423

FACING PAGE **SUZANNE MARSHALL**
Echoing Spring ■ 2012
66 x 53 inches (167.6 x 134.6 cm)
Cotton fabric, cotton-covered polyester thread, polyester
batting, embroidery floss; hand quilted, hand appliquéd
PHOTO BY GARLAND MARSHALL

TED STORM
ElaTED ■ 2012
89½ x 89½ inches (227.3 x 227.3 cm)
Cotton and silk fabrics, cotton thread, perle cotton thread;
hand pieced, hand appliquéd, padded appliquéd,
embroidered, beaded, padded trapunto, hand quilted
PHOTO BY MIKE MCCORMICK

contributors

Aller, Allison Washougal, Washington 398

Allison, Lori Schmitt Mars, Pennsylvania 115, 329

Andersen, Susie L. Cos Cob, Connecticut 286

Anderson, Faye Broomfield, Colorado 59, 146, 335

Anderson, Vicki Culver Rockport, Texas 332

Andrews, Irene McGuire Gallatin, Tennessee 40, 118, 358

Arnold, Mary Vancouver, Washington 252, 256

Arseneault, Nancy C. Tucson, Arizona 47, 171, 338

Atkins, Janet Athens, New York 60

Atkinson, Susan Nottingham, England 56, 252

Aumond-Capone, Vivian Helena Coarsegold, California 320

Bacon, Jenny Maryborough, Victoria, Australia 41, 193

Badger, Marilyn St. George, Utah 53, 112, 169, 240, 331

Balmat, Ludy Maumelle, Arkansas 57

Bardach, Nancy L. Berkeley, California 238

Barnes, Michele A. Keller, Texas 67, 200, 298, 413

Barrett, Barbara Ann Bauer Bastrop, Texas 268

Becka, Diane North Bend, Washington 352

Beebe, Mickey Santa Cruz, California 82, 383, 399

Bergstralh, Jane Williamsburg, Virginia 162, 206, 372

Black, Barbara A. Huntsville, Alabama 54, 117, 158

Blanchard, Joan Leahy West Townsend, Massachusetts 50, 180

Bordelon, Mary Alyce Alexandria, Louisiana 289

Bradley, Cathy Mesquite, Texas 208

Brady, Janice Miller Cedar Park, Texas 63

Brister, Betty L. Bandera, Texas 126

Brown, Christine N. Castle Pines, Colorado 84, 285, 334

Brown, Nancy S. Oakland, California 79, 393

Burge, Shelly Lincoln, Nebraska 251, 313

Burgess, Annette M. Union City, Pennsylvania 366

Burnham, Barbara M. Ellicott City, Maryland 138, 162

Buschauer, Georgina Waltensburg, Vuorz, Switzerland 89, 300

Cameron, Beth Manotick, Ontario, Canada 75, 217

Canny, Hazel Spring, Texas 86, 172, 270

Carlson, Kathleen L. Bridgeton, Missouri 111, 144

Carrico, Lynn W. Denton, Texas 304

Carter, Kathi Vineyard, Utah 157, 293

Catanzarito, Susan Renfrew, Pennsylvania 245, 327

Chiovaro, Jenny Bacliff, Texas 110, 154

Chutchian, Betsy Grand Prairie, Texas 360

Cochran, Janet M. Fort Collins, Colorado 159, 306

Collier, Cynthia League City, Texas 51, 102, 199, 204

Collins, Lawna L. Kamloops, British Columbia, Canada 319

Connally, Pat Midland, Texas 127, 364

Cooper, Dawn Fox Procter, British Columbia, Canada 253, 316, 368, 378, 409

Corder, Carole L. Kettle Falls, Washington 209

Creswell, Patrice Perkins Austin, Texas 168

Cunningham, Kelley Stevensville, Maryland 36

Curley, Margaret Phillips Pittsburgh, Pennsylvania 55, 89, 116, 137, 167, 202

Dague, Susan Piedmont, California 19, 348, 363

Davis, Mary Kay Sunnyvale, California 116, 143

Day, Betty Cawthon Wolfe City, Texas 416

Delaney, Patricia L. Abington, Massachusetts 188, 239, 269, 415

Denneny, Rachelle Glenelg, North Australia, Australia 95

Dickson, Sarah Albright San Antonio, Texas 395

Donohue, Darlene Hilton Head Island, South Carolina 154, 380

Dorsay, Joan Ottawa, Ontario, Canada 235

Doyle, Terri Gilbert, Arizona 272, 274

Drennan, Melba Pearland, Texas 321

Dunklau, Carole J. Manitowoc, Wisconsin 32, 104, 145, 367, 419

Ecob, Aileyn Renli Walnut Creek, California 140

Elking, Leigh Scottsdale, Arizona 134, 382

Erbeck, Kathleen Green Bay, Wisconsin 332

Etienne-Bugnot, Isabelle France 160

Evans, Jerrianne Houston, Texas 43, 64, 202, 368

Everett, Sunny Bellevue, Nebraska 18, 33, 48

Faughnan, Tara Oakland, California 22, 340, 403

Faulkner, Patricia G. Cumberland, Rhode Island 107

Felder, Mary C. Denham Springs, Louisiana 181

Fetterhoff, Margaret "Peggy" The Woodlands, Texas 124, 243

Firth, Dianne Canberra, ACT, Australia 128, 231

Flores, Nona C. Evanston, Illinois 318

Follis, Lynn Cypress, Texas 64, 199

Frydl, Kumiko Houston, Texas 177, 22, 254, 275

Garcia, Cindy Racine, Wisconsin 407

Garman, Susan H. Friendswood, Texas 31, 38, 49, 147, 250

Garrard, Alice Fuchs Redding, Connecticut 113

Goke, Keiko Sendai, Miyagi, Japan 216, 348, 349

Gooding, Hilary Corfe Mullen, Dorset, United Kingdom 93

Graves, Stevii Leesburg, Virginia 298

Grisdela, Cindy Reston, Virginia 81, 347, 355

Guerin, Ewa France 265

Hall, Jane Raleigh, North Carolina 37, 132, 224, 278, 377

Hannah, JoAnn Cleburne, Texas 378, 420

Harrison, Pat Murphy Exeter, Rhode Island 42

Harwell, Ann J. Wendell, North Carolina 337

Hayashi, Naoko Chiba, Japan 91, 150

Mayday, Janet Saddle River, New Jersey 22, 350, 356

Mead, Janice L. Windsor, California 52

Meinisch, Margarete West Hills, California 210, 218

Renshaw, Janet Boyertown, Pennsylvania 195

Hill, Pam Brisbane, Queensland, Australia 17, 94, 361

Hill, Wendy Sunriver, Oregon 119, 408

Hirano, Yukiko (deceased) 10, 142

Holtzman, Barbara Holyoke, Colorado 184

Horton, Ann Redwood Valley, California 309

Huff, Jaynette Conway, Arkansas 65

Huntington, Mary (deceased) 264

Hurley, Leanne Geneva, Illinois 191

Husson, Dominique France 316

Jackson, Gretchen Neal Ann Arbor, Michigan 343

Jackson, Lynette S. Marietta, Georgia 111

Jahn, Barbara Medellin, Columbia 310

Jánosné, Mária Molnár Szekzard, Hungary 120, 137, 284

Johnson, Joanne Sugar Land, Texas 171

Jones, Liz Leominster, Herefordshire, United Kingdom 303

Jones, Susan Deupree New Hartford, Connecticut 74

Judd, Jean M. Cushing, Wisconsin 20, 75

Katsuno, Yachiyo Tokyo, Japan 279, 411

Kerestes, Cheryl Wyoming, Pennsylvania 297

Kerns, Nancy Ellen Laytonsville, Maryland 34

Kido, Noriko Azumino-shi, Nagano, Japan 11, 389

Kiger, Leslie Saint Simons Island, Georgia 73, 387

King, Nancy A. Culver City, California 44, 122

Kitts, Hazel J. Lynchburg, Virginia 267

Knight, Donna Holyoke, Colorado 62

Knorr, Judith Roush Huntington, New York 166

Knowles, Irene Nassau, Bahamas 190

Kobayashi, Yoshiko Katano-City, Osaka, Japan 249, 263, 402

Kolf, Carol Sheridan, Wyoming 180

Korengold, Barbara Chevy Chase, Maryland 102, 149, 197, 198

Kornman, Monna Rowlett, Texas 100

Koseki, Suzuko Tokyo, Japan 317

Kotaki, Mieko Sendai, Japan 270

Kucera, Bonnie Raye Hickman, Nebraska 186, 392

Kuhns, Pat Lincoln, Nebraska 76, 213

Kuroha, Shizuko Suginami-ku, Tokyo, Japan 244

Lacoste, Cecile Blanquefort, France 44

Lambeth, Margie L. Cos Cob, Connecticut 286

Lee, Susan Webb Barnardsville, North Carolina 80, 307

Loeb, Emiko Toda New York, New York 130, 241

Loomis, Diane Sudbury, Massachusetts 121, 184, 234, 276

Lush, Sandie Winterbourne, Bristol, United Kingdom 375

Lyon, Jenny K. Granite Bay, California 183

Machemer, Yolande Corfe Mullen, Dorset, United Kingdom 93

Maddox, Janice Keene Asheville, North Carolina 364

Magee, Sally Heath, Texas 68

Mangum, Vicki Coody Katy, Texas 86, 178, 295

Marigold Appliquérs Chase, British Columbia, Canada 165

Marshall, Suzanne Clayton, Missouri 27, 185, 424

Martin, Judy E. Sheguiandah, Ontario, Canada 228, 361

May, Merry Tuckahoe, New Jersey 68

Mayer, Patricia T. Houston, Texas 260, 308, 400

Mayo, Laurie Emerald Isle, North Carolina 371

McCrady, Kathleen Holland Austin, Texas 15

McCraw, Barbara Ann Denton, Texas 292, 386

McDonald, Margaret Bendigo, Victoria, Australia 39, 72, 388, 414

McLean, Kim Roseville, NSW, Australia 23, 109, 189, 196, 266

McNeil, Kathy Tulalip, Washington 96, 412

Meyer, Gloria Pittsburg, Kansas 115

Miller, Cathleen Albuquerque, New Mexico 173

Milovanova, Olga Kivrov, Vlagimir Region, Russia 107

Miyauchi, Keiko Nagano, Japan 28, 87, 101, 385, 422

Mollon, Sandra L. Valley Springs, California 88, 155, 205, 373

Montgomery, Marian Ann Dallas, Texas 129

Moody, Annie Lima, Ohio 405

Morgenroth, Brigitte Kassel, Germany 259, 403

Morger, Venetta The Woodlands, Texas 187

Morton, Judy Laval Newburgh, Indiana 164, 288, 290

Mowry, Marilyn Ward Irving, Texas 38, 399

Muñoz, Ginger Quinn Colorado Springs, Colorado 322, 357

Myers, Claudia Clark Duluth, Minnesota 55, 229, 257, 295, 339

Nagasawa, Tadako Showa-ku Nagoya, Aichi-ken, Japan 245

New, Betty Naples, Florida 90

Niermann, Petra Melle, Germany 138, 234

Noll, Lynda Marie Cedar Park, Texas 242

Nordstrand, Martha Leesburg, Virginia 298

Nownes, Laura Pleasant Hill, California 12

Oliveira, V'Lou Norman, Oklahoma 358, 394

Ott, Geannine Jacksonville, Arkansas 58

Pagliai, Shelly New Cambria, Missouri 296

Paquin, Gabrielle France 135

Parker, Geri Tulalip, Washington 96, 412

Pearce, Merelyn Jayne Gerroa, NSW, Australia 85, 106, 233, 296, 305

Perejda, Andrea Arroyo Grande, California 83, 174, 274

Pessia, Karen Medford, Massachusetts 184, 375

Peters, Pat Hurricane, Utah 170, 294, 384

Petersen, Ann L. Aurora, Colorado 60, 255

Phelps, Lahala Bonney Lake, Washington 194, 291, 374

Picot, Jocelyne France 203

Pigneri, Ann T. Louisville, Kentucky 276, 351

Plog, Annette Arlington, Texas 301, 306

Rebelo, Beverley Harare, Zimbabwe, Africa 35, 77, 85

Redmond, Wen Strafford, New Hampshire 208, 213, 370

Remick, Helen Seattle, Washington 17, 225, 391

Remmers, Lynda Lima, Ohio 405

Reynolds, Sherry Laramie 126, 141

Riggio, Suzanne Mouton Wauwatosa, Wisconsin 214

Robinson, Kit Fort Collins, Colorado 283

Roger, Penelope Orleans, France 174

Rohrkaste, Rebecca Berkeley, California 311, 336, 346

Rose, Scarlett Anderson, California 366, 418

Round Robin Group Friendswood, Texas 333

Roy, Linda M. Knoxville, Tennessee 50, 144

Russell, Christine M. Manteca, California 261

Saia, Joyce Lyon Beaumont, Texas 342

Saito, Yoko Chiba, Japan 152, 262, 271

Saka, Cristina Sao Paulo, Brazil 33, 179

Sassaman, Jane Harvard, Illinois 20

Schamber, Sharon Payson, Arizona 16, 232, 405

Schipper-Vermeiren, Anna maria Haaften, Netherlands 192, 236, 246, 302

See, Cheryl Ashburn, Virginia 354

Seitz-Krug, Cindy Bakersfield, California 136, 172, 220, 281

Serong, Chris Essendon, Australia 46, 133, 341, 404

Sharkey, Diana Fawn Mt. Kisco, New York 227, 345

Silberman, June F. Ithaca, New York 312

Sirois, Minay Spring, Texas 365

Skjod, Ardie Murrieta, California 182, 324

Smith, Sarah Ann Hope, Maine 251, 280, 285

Snay, Fran Burleson, Texas 123

Solomon, Anita Grossman New York, New York 131, 344

Soules, Jan Elk Grove, California 71, 188

Spahn, Judy Garrison Yellville, Arkansas 226

Spahr, Mary Ellen G. Bluffton, South Carolina 376

Staehle, Carol Arlington, Texas 71, 221, 401

Steadman, Janet Langley, Washington 231

Steele, Linda Park Orchards, Victoria, Australia 13, 108, 176, 410

Stephenson, Becky Fuller Fairfield, Texas 70

Stevenson, Shirley Fowlkes Sherman, Texas 207, 353

Stewart, Susan Pittsburg, Kansas 99, 115, 323

Stipon, Louise-Marie France 92

Stokes, LaRee Meridian, Idaho 76

Stone, Janet Overland Park 147, 151, 310

Stone, Shari L. Houston, Texas 25

Storm, Ted 'S-Gravenzande, Netherlands 223, 421, 425

Sturgill, Nanette L. Salt Lake City, Utah 247

Summerlin, Rahna Walker Port Orange Florida 330, 406

Swanson, Marva M. Atlanta, Georgia 357

Sweet, Holly Cary, North Carolina 69, 143, 326, 362

Tarr, Timna South Hadley, Massachusetts 24, 230, 237, 390

Thackray, Coleen Harare, Zimbabwe, Africa 326

Thompson, Judith Wenonah, New Jersey 21, 98, 114

Thorpe, Zena Chatsworth, California 105, 215, 299, 381, 423

Tignor, Alice Severna Park 120

Tompkins Country Quilters Guild Ithaca, New York 26

Trivedi, Sudha Sugar Land, Texas 34

Tsihlas, Martha Murillo Austin, Texas 219

Turner, Maggie Portland, Oregon 139

Turner, Marline Pietermaritzburg, South Africa 282, 418

Uguen, Anne-Marie France 396

Vail, Madeleine Clark, Colorado 258, 287

Vaine, Janice Jacksonville, Florida 103, 148, 211

Valentine, Gail Centennial, Colorado 300

Verger, Liliane France 161

Verroca, Rita Thousand Oaks, California 14, 30, 369, 379, 417

Veteau, Marie-Josephe France 45, 167

Vierra, Kristin Lincoln, Nebraska 61, 94, 187, 223

Wada, Isako Kurokawa, Miyagi, Japan 153, 325

Walters, Debby Tracy Montgomery, Texas 286

Watkins, Connie Waco, Texas 66, 328

Webb, Christine Montgomeryville, Pennsylvania 81

Weiner, Laurie Clinton, Washington 273, 277

Welsch, Lynn B. Mibres, New Mexico 397

White, Cinzia Gerringong, NSW, Australia 314, 324, 359

Williams, Ramona Bailey Missouri City, Texas 49

Wotruba, David Bremerton, Washington 304

Wrinkle, Georgann Houston, Texas 175, 201, 330, 370

Wylie, Kathy K. Whitby, Ontario, Canada 97, 156, 163

Yokota, Hiromi Yokohama, Kanagawa, Japan 78, 212

Yokoyama, Megumi Nagano, Japan 29, 125

Yoshida, Sachiko Saitama, Saitama, Japan 248, 315

Additional Credits from Contributors

Page 34: *Mary Simon Rediscovered*, Patterns for blocks from D. A. R. Museum (drafted from a quilt in their collection)

Page 47: *An Unexpected Pleasure*, Select appliqué elements from Fandango pattern by Rachel Wetzler

Page 54: *Old Stars, New Day*, Pattern from Stars for a New Day by Sue Garman

Page 56: *Blue Bell Woods*, Adapted from Medallion Coverlet by Martha Jackson, c. 1790-1795

Page 64: *Carrie Hall Sampler*, Adapted from antique blocks by Carrie Hall

Page 66: *Colonial Cockscomb*, Pattern from Simple Blessings by Kim Diehl

Page 67: *Houston County Elegance*, Blocks adapted from antique quilts and Red and Green by Jeni Buechel

Page 68: *Brown Bird's Lullaby*, Little Brown Bird by Margaret Docherty

Page 70: *The Courage Quilt*, Appliqué inspired by From My Heart to Your Hands by Lori Smith, Blocks inspired by Betsey Wright

Page 76: *Emiline*, Inspired by an antique quilt by Emiline Miller

Page 99: *TulipFire*, Inspired by Zundt Designs

Page 115: *Gloria's Garden*, Inspired by Zundt Designs, Piecing adapted from Blooming Nine-Patch from Traditions with a Twist by Blanche Yong and Dalene Young Stone

Page 117: *Joyful Journey*, Pattern from Washington Medallion by Sue Garman

Page 133: *Wrought Iron and Roses*, Roses and leaves inspired by Decorative Flower and Leaf Designs by Richard Hofman, Feather quilting designs modified from The Art of Feather Quilting by Judy Allen

Page 157: *Andrew*, Adapted from More William Morris by Michele Hill

Page 164: *Indiana Starburst*, Inspired by Mary Betsy Toten's 1810 quilt in the Smithsonian Collection

Page 165: *For the Love of Appliqué*, Original Design Using Patterns by Laura Reinstatler, Angela Madden, Scarlett Rose, Faye Labanaris, Anita Shackelford, Emily Senuta, Judy Garden, and Elly Sienkiewicz

Page 170: *Birds and Roses*, Pattern from Birds and Roses by Margaret Docherty

Page 171: *Happy, Happy, Happy*, Select blocks from Country Whig Rose by Kim Diehl

Page 171: *In the Garden with Morris and Hill*, William Morris in Appliqué pattern by Michele Hill

Page 172: *White Orchids*, Inspired by the Orchid Wreath in the International Quilt Festival Collection

Page 178: *Hot Pink Bird's Nest*, Original 3D elements added to patterns by Nancy Pearson

Page 191: *The Wonders of Nature*, Quilt body from Stars in the Garden by Piece O' Cake Designs

Page 200: *Pastorale*, Adapted from Phibe by Di Ford

Page 213: *Timeless Moments*, Appliqué blocks from A Celebration in Appliqué

Page 221: *Fleur de Lis*, Pattern from Blue and White Quilts by Mary Koval

Page 234: *Square in Square I*, Inspired by antique Amish Concentric Squares Quilt in Shelburne Museum, Vermont

Page 235: *Never Again... Again*, Select blocks adapted from designs by Elly Sienkiewicz

Page 242: *Lake Reflections*, Pattern from Tradition with a Twist by Blanche Young and Dalene Young Stone

Page 251: *From the Schooner Coast*, Some pieces from John Flynn's Storm at Sea quilt kit

Page 268: *The Forest and the Trees*, Select blocks adapted from Encyclopedia of Pieced Quilt Patterns by Barbara Brackman

Page 293: *Emily*, Adapted from Conway Album Quilt (I'm Not from Baltimore) by Irma Gail Hatcher's

Page 294: *Hearts and Tulips*, Pattern from Hearts and Tulips by Margaret Docherty

Page 298: *Lapis Vessels*, Inspired by Pat Campbell's books on Jacobean appliqué

Page 304: *Blooms in the B. A.*, Block of the Month by Becky Goldsmith

Page 323: *Radiance*, Inspire by Zundt Designs

Page 338: *Time to Do It!*, Indian Orange Peel pattern by Karen K. Stone

Page 353: *Night Shade*, Inspired by Batik Pineapples by Char Lempke

Page 364: *Stars All Around*, Traditional pattern from Marsha McClosky

Page 366: *President's Wreath*, Based on Homecoming Wreath from Little Quilts All Through the House by Alice Berg, Mary Ellen Von Holt, and Sylvia Johnson

Page 370: *Little Lily*, Adapted from Lily Rosenberry by Sue Garman, Border by Harold Williford

Page 378: *Kootenay Rose*, Inspired by Phoebe Dalrymple (Heritage Quilt Project of New Jersey)

Page 400: *Tribute to Jane*, Variation on design from Dear Jane by Brenda Papadakis

Page 401: *Salute to Salinda*, Pattern from Nearly Insane by Liz Lois

Page 419: *Wisconsin Wedding Quilt*, Design From Wisconsin Quilt Stories in Stitches

About the Juror

Karey Patterson Bresenhan is the president of Quilts, Inc., the director emeritus of the International Quilt Festival, the United States' largest quilt event, and the director of the International Quilt Market, the world's only wholesale tradeshow for the quilting industry. For almost 30 years, Bresenhan owned Great Expectations Quilt Shop in Houston, Texas. A fifth-generation Texas quilter, she is a co-founder of the International Quilt Association and the Alliance for American Quilts and is an honoree named to the Quilters Hall of Fame. In 2011 she co-founded the award-winning Texas Quilt Museum in La Grange, Texas. She is on the national board of the Briscoe Center for American History at the University of Texas and has written nine quilt reference books. Bresenhan holds a bachelor of science degree from Sam Houston State University and a master's degree in journalism from the University of Texas. With her husband, she divides her time between their home near Houston and a ranch near La Grange.

Acknowledgments

- Thanks are due to Vicki Mangum for her invaluable help on the many stages of this book.

- Thanks are due to Amanda Carestio, my editor at Lark, not only for her professionalism and dedication but also for her willingness to first consider, and then implement, a creative new photography plan that truly made this book possible. It was a pleasure to work with you.

- Thanks are also due to Ray Hemachandra, formerly in the crafts division of Lark, for encouraging my idea that there were definitely enough fine art quilts and remarkable traditional quilts for each type to have its own book in the 500 series.

- Finally, heartfelt thanks are due to the quilters who are expanding our view of traditional quilts even as they create extraordinary pieces that honor the tradition itself. I urge all of you—including the legions of talented quiltmakers who could not be included in this book—to keep quilting, to keep creating and stretching your talents to produce those masterpiece quilts, baby quilts, wedding quilts, quilts to give away, quilts to sell, and quilts to comfort when broken hearts need mending. Please continue to grow and to stretch your boundaries. Finally, please remember that there will always be a place for traditional quilts in people's hearts...and on their beds and on their walls and in their museums and in their collections and in their books and in their shows where the traditional quilts win so many awards!

Karey Patterson Bresenha
Director Emerit
International Quilt Festi